Golden Precepts
of Esotericism

Golden Precepts of Esotericism

G. de Purucker

THEOSOPHICAL UNIVERSITY PRESS
PASADENA, CALIFORNIA

THEOSOPHICAL UNIVERSITY PRESS
PASADENA, CALIFORNIA 91109
1979

First Edition published in 1931
Second Edition, Revised, 1935
Third and Revised Edition copyright © 1979
by Theosophical University Press

All rights including the right of reproduction in whole or in part in any form are reserved under International and Pan American Copyright Conventions.

Library of Congress Catalog Card Number 78-74257

Hardcover ISBN 0-911500-85-5
Softcover ISBN 0-911500-86-3

Manufactured in the United States of America

Contents

	Foreword	vii
I	The Path to the Heart of the Universe	1
II	Old Age, Disease, and Death	23
III	The Inner God	69
IV	The Great Heresy of Separateness	91
V	Love is the Cement of the Universe	109
VI	The Chela Path	125
VII	The Buddhas of Compassion	157

Foreword

RECOGNIZING that the "need for esoteric devotional works is probably as great today as it has ever been in the past," G. de Purucker published *Golden Precepts of Esotericism*. This is a small book, yet it deals with large and compelling themes: the path inward to the heart of being; thoughts and their influence on character; how to meet suffering, old age, and death; the potency of love, self-forgetful love, that encompasses the whole of mankind; and, lastly, the choice that every aspirant faces: whether to undergo the higher discipline and training for self-benefit alone, or for the sake of bringing light and wisdom to every living being on earth.

The first edition, issued in 1931, comprised excerpts taken from public lectures and private talks given by Dr. de Purucker during the first two years of his leadership of the Theosophical Society (1929-42) and arranged in dialogue form by G.B., a friend and student of the author. In 1935, in response to requests from readers abroad and in the United States, Dr. de Purucker brought out a second edition in which the questions were omitted and the teaching presented in narrative form. The book went through numerous reprintings and was translated into several European languages. The present volume follows closely this second edition as revised by the author.

It was Dr. de Purucker's hope that others would be "illumined with the same light and receive the same inspiration" that he himself had received from a lifelong absorption in the ideals and teachings of the Mystery Schools.

GRACE F. KNOCHE

June 21, 1979
Pasadena, California

The Path to the Heart of the Universe

I

The Path to the Heart of the Universe

THERE is a hunger in every human heart, which nothing can satisfy or appease — a hunger for something more true than ordinary human beings wit of, a hunger for the real, a hunger for the sublime. It is the nostalgia of the soul, of the spirit-soul of man. The source of this longing is the homesickness brought about by the soul-memory of our spiritual abode, whence we came and towards which we are now on our return journey.

Men unconsciously, intuitively, unknown to the brain-mind, see the vision sublime on the mountaintops of the mystic East; and oh! this yearning homesickness for the indescribable, for the immortal, for the deathless, for that which brings unutterable peace and a love which is frontierless in its reaches! Every human heart feels this, and it is the saving power in men, the thing which gives them hope and aspiration, which raises their souls with the recognition of the glory that once was theirs.

Light for the mind, love for the heart, understanding for the intellect: all three must be satisfied in every man before he has real peace.

There is a path, a sublime pathway of wisdom and illumination which begins, for each human being, in any one incarnation on this earth in the present life, and thereafter leads inward, for it is the pathway of consciousness and spiritual realization leading ever inward, more inward, still more inward, toward the mystic East, which is the heart of the universe, and it is the core of you — the rising sun of spiritually divine consciousness within you.

Every faculty, energy, everything, is in the core of the core of your being, which is your road, so to speak, by which you grow out from the heart of Being, which is your spiritual selfhood.

The path to the heart of the universe is one and yet different for every human being. The meaning is that every human being himself is that pathway — that pathway which is builded of thought and consciousness and of the fabric of your own being. It is builded of the stuff of nature's heart.

There is a long road; it is also broad. It is the road whereon you have nature's streaming current of energy with you, and following this road you will reach perfection in due time; but this is the road of long-enduring slow evolution, moving ahead little by little in each life, through the incalculable ages.

There is another road, steep and thorny, difficult to follow, but which the Great Ones of the human race have trodden. It is the quick road, but the difficult one. It is the road of self-conquest, the road of the giving up of self for the All, the road by which the personal man becomes the impersonal Buddha, the impersonal Christ; the road by which the love for your own is abandoned, and your whole being becomes filled with love for all things both great and small. It is a difficult road to follow, for it is the road of initiation; it is the steep and thorny pathway to the gods; for when you climb the heights of Olympus you must tread the pathway as there it lies before you.

In the Orient there have been from immemorial time four paths* which the four classes or types of men, according to this ancient theory of Hindustan, follow.

The first is *karma mārga,* the "path of action" — salvation by works.

The second is *bhakti mārga,* the "path of devotion" — salvation by faith.

These two paths or these two systems of

---

*These four pathways correspond very accurately with the four grades, social and political, of the early civilizations of Hindustan in the Vedic period: the *śūdra,* the agriculturist; the *vaiśya,* the commercial man; the *kshattriya,* the administrator, the warrior, the king, the prince, in short, the world of officialdom, etc.; and fourth, the *brāhmana,* the philosopher, the sage.

improving the heart and mind of men are also more or less known in the Occident, and have been respectively called salvation by works, and salvation by faith. But these two paths are not the highest.

The third path is *rāja-yoga mārga,* the "path of rāja-yoga": the path which the striving entity follows in order to attain freedom and light; to attain that real union with the self within by means of self-devised efforts. And the fourth path, considered to be for the choicest of men, was called *jñāna mārga,* the "wisdom path": the path of the great seers and sages and, generally speaking, of the noblest portion of mankind.

Beautiful are the pathways, sublime the goal, and quick the feet of them who follow the way of the still, small voice within, which way leadeth to the heart of the universe. This is the core of the messages of the great Mysteries of antiquity — the union of the simple human being with his divine source, with the root of himself, linked as that is with the All, for that core is a spark of the central

Fire, a spark of divinity; and this spark is in everyone.

Divinity is at the heart of you. It is the root of you. It is the core of the core of your being; and you can ascend along the pathway of the spiritual self, passing veil after veil of obscuring selfhood, until you attain unity with that inner divinity. That is the most sublime adventure known to man — the study of the self of man.

Thus you will climb the mountains not merely of Parnassus and of Olympus, but you will in time, by following this inner pathway of self-knowledge, grow so greatly in understanding and in inner vision, that your eyes will take in ranges and sweeps of inner light, unveiling to you the most awful, because the holiest and the most beautiful, mysteries of the boundless universe.

The first step on the pathway to the heart of the universe is to recognize the truth that all comes from within. All the inspirations of genius, all the great thoughts which have made and unmade civilizations, all the wonderful messages that have been delivered by the Great Ones of the earth to their fellow human beings — all these come forth from within. The battle of union, towards union, for union, with your own inner god, is more than half won when you recognize this truth.

How splendid is the pathway seen after that! How glorious is it! Leading ever more inward and inward, which is the same as saying upward and upward, ever higher and higher, till you become at one with your own kin — the gods — who are the governors and rulers of the universe, and of whom men are the children.

The inmost of the inmost of you is a god, a living divinity; and from this divine source there flow downwards into your human mentality all the things that make men great, all the things that give rise to love and mighty hope and inspiration and aspiration, and noblest of all, self-sacrifice.

In yourself lie all the mysteries of the universe. Through your inner self, your spiritual nature, you have a road reaching to the very heart of the universe. If you travel that road leading ever within, if you can go into yourself, go behind veil after veil of selfhood, deeper and deeper into yourself, you go deeper and deeper into the wondrous mysteries of universal nature.

Knowing yourself, you progress more quickly than the average running of the evolutionary course; and when this pace is quickened to the utmost, there are initiations, short cuts in fact, but only for those who are fit and ready to take these difficult, very difficult, short cuts. Growth proceeds step by step.

This pathway is spoken of as a road, yet it is the unlocking of the heart of man — not the physical heart, but the heart of his being, the essence of the man; in other words the unlocking and development of his spiritual and intellectual and psychical powers and faculties. This is the doctrine of the heart, the secret doctrine, the doctrine which is hid. The eye doctrine is that which can be seen and is more or less open.

Those whose inner faculties and powers have come more into actual operation and into conscious functioning, whose inner natures have been more developed, as they grow from childhood towards manhood, in any one life, are the fit, the neophytes, whose natures are opening, and who have the ears to hear and the eyes to see what is put before them.

Those who have the intuition of something greater within, of something splendid and grand, of something which is growing within the heart and within the mind, like the budding flower: these are the ones who shall finally see more; these are the initiates developing into the great seers and sages.

There is no favoritism in nature. The old, old rule is a true one. Man takes what he himself can get — *what he himself is.*

Man is an inseparable part of the universe in which he lives and moves and has his being. There is no separation whatsoever between his roots and the roots of the universe, there is no distance between them.

The same universal life flows through all things that are. The same stream of consciousness which flows in the mighty Whole and through the mighty Whole of the universe, flows therefore through man, an inseparable portion of that universe. This means that there is a pathway by which you may come into intimate relation with the heart of the universe itself; and that pathway is you, your own inner being, your own inner nature, your spiritual self. Not the self of ordinary physical man, which self is just a poor reflection of the spiritual brilliance within, but that inner self of pure consciousness, pure love for all that is, unstained by any earthly taint — your spiritual being.

Following this pathway to your own inner god, your higher self, you will reach all the mysteries and wonders of boundless infinitude, through infinite time; and such happiness and peace and bliss and beauty and love and inspiration will fill your whole being that every breath will be a blessing, and every thought a sublime inspiration.

How can one live the life so as to advance on this pathway? A clean heart, a pure mind, an eager intellect, the searching to obtain an unveiled spiritual perception: these are the first steps of the golden stairs, ascending which you will pass into nature's temple of wisdom. This "living the life" has naught to do with foolish asceticism, such as torturing the body, and all such vain and self-destructive methods. Not at all.

There is a totally wrong idea in the world that the way to obtain the "kingdom of heaven" (to use the ordinary Christian phraseology) is by giving up your manhood; that the way to grow strong is by becoming a fool; and that the way to attain divine peace and harmony is by becoming an imbecile on the earth. The so-called ascetic is on the wrong path. A man will never attain the kingdom of heaven merely by living on potatoes and carrots, or by sleeping only half an hour a day or night, or by lying on a bed of spikes, or by abstaining from this and doing that merely with the physical body.

Oh, the picture that I have seen of men subduing the body, as they thought, and yet with minds crooked and degraded with corruption! Wickedness is not in the body; evildoing is not of the body. The body is an irresponsible instrument of your will and of your intelligence. It is your will and your intelligence which you must train; and then you train yourselves and you become truly men and are on the pathway to human divinity.

Do not kill your personality; do not annihilate your personality in the sense of wiping it out. You have brought it into being yourself; it is a part of you, the emotional and psychical part of you, the lower mental part of you, the passional part of you, the evolutionary work of aeons upon aeons in the past. Raise the personality. Cleanse it, train it, make it shapely and symmetrical to your will and to your thought, discipline it, make it the temple of a living god so that it shall become a fit vehicle, a clean and pure channel for passing into the human consciousness the rays of glory streaming from the god within — these rays of glory being rays of consciousness of the spirit, of the spiritual or divine consciousness.

It is not the fall of the personal which frees the spiritual man; it is the raising of the personal into becoming spiritual, which is the work of evolution. This is the same thing that natural evolution in its slow age-long process is trying to accomplish — to raise the lower up to become higher — not to kill it, not to down it.

Be the holiest and noblest and purest that you can think of. Then you can forget your body. You can forget your personality which the body expresses; and by personality I mean all the lower faculties of you: the lower mental and the emotional part of you, your whims and your little this and little that. Salvage your lower portions to nobler and superior uses.

When the personal shall have become transfigured; when the personal shall be able to manifest more or less fully the sublime inflow from the god within you — your own inner, spiritual-divine splendor — then you will walk the earth like a human god, and act like a god. For each one is the representation on earth of his own inner god, and you represent on the physical sphere as much of the divine essence streaming through your being as your evolution permits you to manifest. Therefore, begin even now to express the god within. You can, and the reward that comes from this is unspeakably grand and beautiful.

In proportion as you ally yourself with your own inner god, with the fountain of divinity which is constantly pouring through your own inner being, does your consciousness ascend and expand in power and reach, so that with inner growth comes expanding vision on the one hand and the expanding consciousness to interpret that vision on the other hand.

Turn your gaze inward, not outward; and this does not mean to be solely introspective and to abandon extraspection. That is not the idea. You must see in both directions. But do not seek for truth in any place except in the faculty which cognizes truth which is your inmost self, for it alone can cognize truth.

It is the active brain-mind, filled with thoughts of the day, filled with desires of the hour, filled with the prejudices and opinions which are so transitory — and which more than anything else this active brain-mind is afflicted with — which prevent your visioning of the truth, prevent your obtaining the vision sublime.

You cannot know truth except with the knower; you cannot understand anything outside of you except with and by and through the understander within you; and yet what is outside of you is likewise within you, for you are an inseparable part of the universe, of which you are a child. Every entity is an inseparable part of the boundless All, because he is its offspring, its child, so to speak, life of its life, blood of its blood, thought of its thought. And the way to obtain the vision sublime, and to see that vision sublime growing ever more sublime forever, is by looking within, following the still, small pathway of the inner consciousness. This is what is meant by the injunction: Man, know thyself!

Nothing then will mislead you, nothing then can mar or change what you are in your heart of hearts; for divinity will be fighting for you, divinity will carry your burdens. Where now your heart is torn and rent in pain and sorrow, so that oft you know not whither to turn, then shall peace and love come stealing into your heart and will guide, will enlighten, because they will illuminate, your pathway unto the gods, which pathway is yourself, your divine self, which is rooted in the divinity at the heart of things. Follow that pathway until you enter into the life of the cosmic divine as a self-conscious god.

The way by which to find this path, the manner of approach to it, is self-forgetfulness, just as when on the distant mountain peaks you see the dawn, and all things small and personal fall away from you. It is the self-forgetful man who is great; it is the self-forgetful woman who is sublime. Self-forgetfulness (marvelous paradox!) is the way to find the self divine.

Every faculty of man's nature must be brought into activity in this high and sublime work. No imperfect entity can climb the heights of Parnassus; no human can ascend the peaks of Olympus unless he himself be a near-god, developing into godhood from manhood.

Therefore the intellectual faculty, being one of the noblest in the human inner constitution, also must be developed. There must be understanding as well as feeling. Both are necessary. When you have these two conjoined and sympathetically cooperating, you have the sage, the seer. You cannot reach the heights leaving part of yourself below in the valleys. You must go up — the whole of you. Train your mind; train your will; train your heart; train your intelligence.

When you turn to your greater self, which is the higher part of your own constitution; when you become the inner Buddha, when you become the Christ within you, although you give up the physical personality and the mental personality and the crippling things which distract you and worry you and cause you to fret and give you pain and sorrow, you enter into the sublime light of the spirit, and exchange the personality for divinity. It is worth giving up everything to attain it, for when a man gives up his life for the sake of the Christ within him he shall find it, because in so doing he finds the life universal.

In doing this you renounce nothing of intrinsic and real value. You give up nothing that is worthy and fine and noble. What you do is to throw off the shackles, the chains, that bind your interior faculties. What you do is to take the first steps into freedom and light.

Who would willingly remain in a dungeon? Give up your personal, lower, material self, your selfish life on this gross physical plane, and then you will begin to sense the existence of the life everlasting, with all its concomitant wisdom and power, and all the increase in faculty and vision that will then accrue to you. When you succeed in doing this, then indeed you will have the vision sublime.

There in the distant mystic East, on the mountain peaks of the spirit, you will see the rising sun. You yourself will enter into light and freedom. You will be subject to the dicta of none, controlled by none; you will be a free man: free in the spirit, free of intellect, because you will have become one with spiritual nature. You will have entered into the temple of the holy one within your own heart of hearts, and there, in the adytum, you will see your own inner god.

How wonderful, holy, sublime, inspiring as none other, is this truth: that within each one there is an unspeakable fount of strength, of wisdom, of love, of compassion, of forgiveness, of purity! Ally yourself with this fountain of strength; it is in you, none can ever take it from you. Its value is more excellent than all the treasures of the universe, for knowing it, being it, you are All.

For one bright intelligence pervades all things; and what is in the star is in the flower under our feet; and it is the instinctive recognition of this thing of beauty which has led the poet to speak of the flower as a star of beauty. The same life force pours through it as through the star; the same bright flame of intelligence gives to it its exquisite form, shape, color, and this is the same bright flame of intelligence that controls the passing of the stars along their cosmic ways.

Old Age, Disease, and Death

II

Old Age, Disease, and Death

HOW beautiful is the world that surrounds us! The sunrise over the eastern mountaintops is one of the most exquisitely beautiful things I know.

It is so beautiful because it calls forth within us a harmony of understanding akin to the natural beauty which we see painted on the eastern sky. All beauty is in the consciousness of the perceiver therefore, where, in a very true sense, all things that we cognize are.

You cannot see beauty outside unless you have beauty within you. You cannot understand beauty unless you yourself are beautiful inside. You cannot understand harmony unless you yourself in your inner parts are harmony. All things of value are within yourself, and the outside world merely offers you the stimulus, the stimulation, of and to the exercise of the understanding faculty within you.

There is beauty in understanding, and understanding springs only from an understanding heart, paradoxical as that may sound at first hearing. It is the understanding heart that has vision.

The seer trains himself to open the seeing eye, and nature speaks to him in tones which grow with each year more entrancing, more wonderful, because he is growing greater inside. His understanding is broadening and deepening. The whispering of the trees, the susurrus of the leaves and their rustling, the slow boom of the waves on the shingle of the shore, the chirp of the cricket, the cooing of the dove, the sound of a human voice — strident though oft it is — contain marvels for him. He recognizes his kinship with all that is, he realizes that he is but one element in a most marvelous mosaic of life in which he is inseparably bound, and that even as the

OLD AGE, DISEASE, AND DEATH 27

vision grows it becomes ever more beautiful and sublime; and he knows that the vision sublime is there, and strives to see it ever more clearly.

Every tree, every flower, every atom of the mineral crunched under your feet as you tread the surface of the earth, everything that is, had you the seeing eye, you could learn from. Have you never looked into the bosom of a flower? Have you never studied the beauty, symmetry, glory, around you? Have you never looked at the rising or the setting sun and marveled at the paintings on the eastern or western horizon? Have you never looked deep into the eye of a fellow human being, looked with a seeing eye on your own kind? Have you never found marvels there? What a wonderful world we are surrounded by! Yet with all the beauty surrounding us, the heart aches and the mind is overwhelmed with the thought of the woes of mankind caused by the three dire problems — old age, disease, and death.

Learn to control the mind. Man is a child

28 OLD AGE, DISEASE, AND DEATH

of the gods, and his mind should be godlike, his thoughts aspiring, his heart constantly opening in love ever more; and therefore his attitude should be godlike also.

Go into the silent places of your heart; enter into the chambers so quiet and still of your inner being. Soon you will learn to knock at the doors of your own heart. Practice makes perfect. Intuition will then come to you. You will have knowledge immediately; you will know truth instantly. That is the Way; that is the teaching.

In these silent places you receive illumination, you receive visions of truth, because your spirit — the core of you, the heart of you — has gone into the very core of being, where it is native, from which it is separated never, from which it originally sprang, and with which you are in direct and unceasing communication.

Realize this wonderful truth; take it to heart. For there are fountains inexhaustible of wisdom, of knowledge, and of love — yes, and power — power over self first of all, which means power over nature, in which we live and move and have our being. For the core of your being is the inner god in you, the divine spirit, the Christos-spirit, the Buddhic splendor.

It is into these quiet places of the soul, into these deep silences of the heart — that is to say, the inmost of the inmost of the human being — that enter the Great Ones when they want to acquire more light and greater knowledge; for by so doing they enter into the very structure and fabric of the universe, and therefore know truth at first hand, because they become in their own minds and intelligences — in the interpreting organ we call the mentality — one with that universe, vibrating synchronously, sympathetically, with the vibrations on all planes of the Eternal Mother. There they become at one with All, and therefore know truth intuitively.

Old age need have no fears for you. One who has lived aright, one who has lived cleanly, and thought highly, as age comes on him and the body weakens and the physical veils thin, sees, and seeing knows. His vision passes behind the veils of matter, for he is slowly becoming acquainted with the mysteries beyond the veil which men call death.

For a certain period of time, dependent upon the interval preceding death, the soul is withdrawing from the aged body. This accounts for the so-called advance in the symptoms and physical phenomena of age, of old age. But such withdrawal of the soul, in the normal course, is peaceful and quiet, and is nature's way of making death come as a quiet blessing of peace and harmony.

Death is birth, *birth;* and instead of the wrench that there actually is in the case of youth when death comes, death to our old ones comes in peace and quiet, stealing like an angel of mercy into their being, releasing the bonds binding the soul to its vehicle of flesh; and the passage is as quiet and gentle as the coming of the twilight preceding night, and it is a blessed sleep.

Any human being can avoid a painful old age, or at least very largely modify its troubles; and this can be attained by living humanly, by living in your higher self, instead of idealizing the wants and desires of your body. Then old age comes stealing upon you, bringing blessings with it, and increase in all the higher faculties and powers; so that the approach of old age is vibrant with the harmonies of another world, and beautiful with its visions of truth and glory.

Old age is a blessing, if the previous life has been lived aright. It brings with it things otherwise unattainable, such as an expansion of consciousness which youth knows nothing of. It brings with it increased intellectual power which, because of its very reach, the undeveloped person, the youth, the man of middle age, does not understand, and therefore ascribes to the vague generalizations of grandfather. Grandfather in such circumstances is nearer the truth and sees more than does the still unseeing eye of the youth. A fine old age brings an expansion of soul, not only of the intellect, but of the spiritual consciousness and its vision.

But sometimes, when the life has been lived in gross physical desires; when, so to say, the bonds uniting the soul to the body have been riveted into the vehicle of flesh by self-indulgence in the gross appetites, then even in age death is painful; for the natural withdrawal of the soul has not taken place, or at least not to such a large degree, nor is the physical age attained so great before death finally comes.

Old age is nothing to fear. It is a blessing. It is a splendor seen as through a veil, of the life beyond, the higher life, the life in which the higher incarnating ego lives, literally. Shadows — coming events casting their shadows before, the shadows of the splendor to be — such is a fine old age.

Diseases, the second of the woes that afflict mankind, are purifying processes, processes of purification, and to men of our present imperfect stage of evolution, in many, many instances are a heaven-sent blessing. They cure egoism. They teach patience. They

OLD AGE, DISEASE, AND DEATH 33

bring about in their train a dwelling of the mind on the beauty of life, on the need for living rightly. They make one kindly and sympathetic.

Consider the average man in his present imperfect stage of evolution: passionate, with ungoverned emotions, with fierce desires for sensation, for ever more sensation, and still more sensation. Consider a moment if men of today, such as they are, had bodies which could not be diseased, but could be weakened and killed by excesses. Do you not see that things as they are have a very kindly side to them? Diseases actually are our warnings to reform our evil thoughts and to live in accordance with nature's laws.

Remember that it is not an outside and tyrannical nature which brings disease upon us; disease is in every instance the result or consequence of our own wrongdoing: mental wrongdoing, and physical wrongdoing: either in this or in some past life. Diseases, with their concomitant suffering and pain, are our best monitory friends. They soften our hearts, they broaden our minds, they give us an opportunity for the exercise of our wills and a field for the play of our moral instincts. They also instill pity and compassion for others in our breasts.

It is true that each one of us is responsible for his diseases and his misfortunes; all the misfortunes of life we ourselves have made for ourselves. We have deserved them, because we are the parents of them. They come upon us, we ourselves receive them, and are merely receiving the reaction, the effects, of the seeds of thought and act that we have sown in the past — a wonderful doctrine, karma!

Yet "good" and "bad" are relative. We call things good when they happen to please us, and when we do not like them, we say that they are bad. And yet the very thing or things which at the time you did not like in some cases have turned out splendidly for you, brought you good luck, brought you happiness, at the very least put strength of fiber into your character, which is worth more

OLD AGE, DISEASE, AND DEATH 35

than all worldly treasures. They gave you insight, unlocked the powers of your heart, enabled you to think; in short, made a man of you.

Nothing happens to us which we ourselves did not engender in the beginning. We sowed the seeds. Now the seeds have grown up in us, and we say: I cannot understand how such a thing could have happened to me. But it has happened, and if you take it rightly and face it rightly, and react properly, and look upon it as just the thing that you would have chosen, you become a collaborator with destiny, and become happy, and grow. Strength becomes yours. Wisdom grows in your heart.

Let me illustrate with the case of an exceedingly good and noble man. Suddenly he is stricken, let us say, to make the case picturesque and pointed, with some loathsome and terrible disease. Nothing in his present life that he knows of has brought this about. He is suddenly and unaccountably stricken down, so that, for a while, he hates himself, and his soul turns in agony to the gods who hear not, and he says: "What have I done to bring this thing upon me?" Shall we say that he is a bad man? No, he is a good man; but this is a case where past seeds, seeds of thought, of emotion, of weakness, in past lives had hitherto not yet eventuated, hitherto had not come to fruitage, but now do so. Now they come forth. In past lives perhaps they wanted to come forth and the man was a coward and dammed them back, in some way or other by thought, postponing the agony until some later day.

The lesson of this, therefore, is: when misfortune comes upon you, when sorrow racks your heart, and when it seems as if all the world had turned against you, then be a man. Face it all, and have done with it; so that, in the future, when your character is stronger and more improved, you shall not have laid up for yourself some unworked-out seed of karmic destiny then to blossom and bring you greater unhappiness by far than it could now bring.

OLD AGE, DISEASE, AND DEATH 37

There have been great and noble men, disciples on the path, and advanced at that, to whom such occurrences have happened. Old karmic seeds of destiny, held over, dammed back, willed to disappear — now coming forth and apparently ruining a noble life.

So when sorrow comes, when grief appears in your life, when pain comes upon you, take them to your heart; for they are the awakeners. Pleasures lull you to sleep; the so-called joys send you to sleep. It is sorrow, it is grief, it is change which you do not like — it is precisely these three things which are your awakeners. Seize the truth of this! It will give you strength; it will give you peace; it will enable you to meet the problems of life with an illuminated mind; it will bring you help and comfort.

Remember, it is only the finite which suffers; likewise it is the finite which loves. It is the finite which does these, because it learns. It is learning, growing; no matter how small it may be, no matter how great — insect and god, supergod and atom of earth — all are learning and growing, therefore passing through stages of happiness and bliss, and of suffering and pain.

Everything that *is* is an opportunity to the percipient eye and the understanding heart to learn, which means to grow; and when you realize that suffering and pain are two of the means by which we grow, then come peace to the heart and rest to the mind.

What is it that makes the majestic oak such as it is? Is it the gentle zephyr and the soft-pattering rain? The oak might be weak and yielding as a willow to the blast if that were the truth. No, the tempest and the storm have their way with the oak, and the oak reacts in robustness and strength; battling the storm and tempest it grows strong.

Human beings learn far more quickly than does the so-called insensate plant. There is nothing that learns so quickly and easily as does the human heart. Therefore shrink not from suffering and pain, for they are better teachers than are happiness and smug contentment. The latter is almost spiritually suicidal — to be so smugly content with yourself and what you are that you sleep. But nature will not have it thus always. Finally there comes the karmic impulse, the karmic stimulus, and then you suffer a little; but in doing so you awaken and begin to grow. Bless the karmic stimulus; be not afraid of it. Look to the essential divinity within. Remember that everything that happens is transient, and that you can learn from everything, and in learning you will grow — grow great, and from greatness pass to a larger sphere of greatness.

It is all a battle of self against self: not exactly a fighting each other, but nevertheless a constant enduring against odds, and this is, in a way, a spiritual exercise. It is exercise that makes us strong, that makes us lithe and vigorous, ready to face still greater trials and difficulties. The greatest friend that we have, the noblest cleanser of all, is sorrow, or is pain, for the heart and mind must be cleansed by pain even as gold is tried in the fire.

We humans ordinarily do not like this. In that respect we are just like little children; but nevertheless the fact is so, and we soon learn, when we become thoughtful, that the real man faces the trials and difficulties of life in a joyous mood, and conquers.

A beautiful, helpful rule is the following: whatever comes to you, meet it manfully. Look upon it as the very thing that you would have willed — and therefrom reap peace. It will pass, it will work itself out. It is a good practical rule of the moral law: repine not, keep your face to the mystic East of the future, fill your heart with courage, and remember that you are a descendant of and kin to the immortal gods who control and guide the universe.

There are times indeed in life when the higher self actually leads us into paths of trial so that we may grow by reacting successfully against the trials. But the higher self is always with us, constantly warning us in the shape of intimations and intuitions to be courageous, to face life boldly, to be truthful, to be clean, to be strong, to be sincere, to be upright, and many other such things; and these precisely are the very qualities in human nature which, when followed out continuously, protect us against disaster. The only real disaster that the spirit-soul of man knows is weakness, is failure, is discouragement. Physical disasters and other things of physical life are often blessings in disguise; the higher self teaches us how to meet these in the proper mood, and how best to come forth from them triumphant.

It is the inner joy which carries us on to victory, the sense of feeling that we cannot achieve before we *will* to do it; and this could not be unless the very heart of the universe were harmony and love, for the heart of things is celestial peace and love and beauty.

Therefore, when pain and suffering come upon you, remember these truths. Stand up! Be a man! Face the storm; and before you know it you will see the blue sky ahead, and success and prosperity, because you have acted like a man. You have passed through

42 OLD AGE, DISEASE, AND DEATH

the test, and it has made you the stronger.

All physical maladies have their ultimate origin in a faulty outlook on life, in a faulty direction taken by the individual will. All diseases therefore ultimately, not as they exist when once they exist in the physical body and wreak their work of suffering and pain, but as they exist in their origin, have this origin in the mind — in this or another life. Weakness of will, the giving way to bad habits breeding seeds of thought which leave thought-deposits in the mind, enfeeble the character. An evil or false thought manifests in a body and ultimately ruins it by bad habits. And criticism, pessimism, and the habit of making complaints and faultfinding are diseases of the mind in very truth.

Every sage and seer has taught the same thing: cleanse the temple of the holy spirit, drive out the demons of the lower nature. What are these demons? One's own thoughts.

Inharmonious thoughts not only poison the air, but they also poison your very blood-

OLD AGE, DISEASE, AND DEATH 43

stream, poison your body; and disease is the resultant. What are inharmonious thoughts? They are selfish thoughts, evil thoughts, mean thoughts, thoughts out of tune; and they arise in a heart which lacks love. Perfect love in the human heart tends to build up a strong body, physiologically clean, because the inside of you is psychologically and morally clean, harmonious in its workings, for in this case, the mind, the soul, the spirit — the true man — are harmonious in their workings. The body merely reflects what you are.

You are making yourself now very largely what you will be ten years from now. You may have conquered a disease that you are now suffering from. You may have a disease then that now you have not. In either case you are yourself responsible. The greatest preventive of disease is a selfless soul working through a selfless mind — a self-forgetful heart. Nothing brings disease upon a human being so quickly as selfishness with its concomitant temptations, and the succumbing to those temptations. Be utterly unselfish, and the world's wealth is yours: wealth of health, wealth of vision, of physical riches, wealth of power, wealth of love, wealth of faculty, wealth of everything.

When the thoughts chase through the mind as unruly steeds, do not struggle and waste your force. Picture to yourself the things opposite to those you hate. Picture the things that you really inwardly love, really love in your heart, and which you know are helpful. The secret is inner visualization: therefore visualize.

If you find yourself gloomy, if you are ashamed of thoughts that are in your mind, do not struggle with them, do not fight them, forget them. They are only ghosts rising out of your own past. But turn your head to the East and watch the rising sun. Paint the visions in glory. Watch the mountaintops of your nature where rosy-fingered Aurora of the inner dawn weaves the web of her splendorous magic before your eyes.

There you have the secret of conquest. This is the best way, the easiest way, and you can follow it because you are the creator of your own destiny through your imagination and will power. By doing this the creative faculty within you comes into operation. This is so simple a rule and yet it is the message of the sages of the ages.

Forget the evil thoughts and do not give them an artificial life by visualizing them and then fighting them. Do not waste your energies in fighting bogies, the phantoms and ghosts of your imagination. These are only the phantasms of your own imagination, and have no reality outside of yourself. Yet these phantoms and ghosts can at times overcome you and become a temporary reality because you have given them the framework and power of thought. You incarnate these things in thoughts, and thoughts will govern your body.

Visualize the other thing. Make pictures of beauty and strength in your mind. If you are obsessed by these uglinesses, picture to yourself scenes of beauty. It is far more fascinating. It is a delightful pastime, and it always works. See things of a high and noble character and visualize them forcefully. Visualize to yourself a success in fine things. Visualize things of beauty, of inward splendor.

The mind can be raised with high and noble thoughts. Even the worker, while his hands are busy, can trace his ancestry in thought to the gods in space, and feel the inspiration of a divine ancestry flowing through the veins of his soul, so to speak. He can thereby be truly a man.

Silence your thoughts: this does not mean to stop thinking, but to control your thoughts, be the master of them. Do not be the slave of the vagrant mental tramps that run through your mind. Give birth to thoughts and rule these your children, and when they become naughty put the dampers on. Silence them.

Be a thinker, not so much of thoughts, as of thought. In other words, leave the restless activity of your brain-mind, and go into the inner chambers of your heart, into the recesses of your consciousness, the holy place within, and see the light. Receive the light. Silence

OLD AGE, DISEASE, AND DEATH 47

your thoughts, and enter into consciousness.

Examine your own mental processes, and see how much time you waste in merely thinking thoughts, useless thoughts most of them, and neglect to drink of those sublime fountains of knowledge and wisdom and consciousness that you have within you, the sources of inspiration and genius — to drink of the genial springs, of those Pierian founts, whence flows all that makes life worth while.

There is a test by which one can make certain whether something that springs into the mind comes from the higher self, or whether it is merely from some desire or colored by some desire. Here is your test, and an easy one. The higher self is impersonal; it is self-forgetful; it is kind; it is loving; it is pitiful; it is compassionate; it has sublime inspirations. The lower nature is selfish, ingathering, acquisitive for self, hateful often, unforgiving, violent.

The higher self is a spiritual entity and, so to say, soars above the mud of the lower self much as the sun shines upon the earth.

48 OLD AGE, DISEASE, AND DEATH

The higher self has tremendous influence on the lower self; but the lower self has no influence whatever, not even indirect, on the higher self. The lower self has tremendous influence on the human self, however, the intermediate nature.

If what comes wandering into your mind, or is brought thither by your own will power and aspiration, is such as urges you to do good to your fellow men, gives you inner peace and comfort, makes you kindlier and more thoughtful of others, it is from the higher part. This higher impulse may be a desire, but it is not a desire for the personality; it is a desire of the spirit, a desire to grow greater, to be more, to help others, to love, to forget injury, to forgive.

A kindly thought sent out towards some other human being is a protection to that other, and it is a beautiful thing to do. It is a human thing, a truly human thing, and one that every normal human being loves to do. There are few things so satisfying to both heart and mind as the feeling that, today at

OLD AGE, DISEASE, AND DEATH 49

least, we have not been unkind in our feelings or thoughts towards others, but have been helpful, kindly, considerate, impersonal.

The sowing of the seeds of thought is not an act devoid of responsibility. Anyone who sows seeds of thought in the minds of his fellow men is held by natural law to a strict accountability. Nature is not anarchic; it is governed by cause and effect throughout — by karma.

While this places a serious responsibility upon anyone who teaches others, and who thus puts seeds of thought and feeling into their minds, nevertheless, on the other hand, what is the guerdon of a noble work well done? The reward, the recompense, is magnificent.

Guard well your thoughts, and even as carefully guard what you say. Speak little, but when you do speak, speak with deliberate recollection of your responsibility.

What is a thought? A thought is a thing: it is a living entity. All the vast and diversified phenomena of nature, so far as differentiations are concerned, are founded upon the one fact that at the heart of each such entity there exists a thought divine, a seed of the divine, which is destined to grow through the aeons until the inherent life, individuality, power, and faculty, in such a seed shall find itself flowing forth into more or less perfect manifestation. It is thus that such a god-seed or monad becomes in its turn a divine entity, a self-conscious god, a child of the cosmic divine, its parent.

Thoughts are things, because thoughts are substantial. Thoughts are substantial entities — not composed of the substance of our physical world, but of ethereal substance, etheric substance.

Man is a focus of creative powers; he is a focus of energies constantly throwing forth from himself innumerable streams, rivers, of little lives. Through his physical emanations, these atomic lives, these life-atoms, leave him. Through his mind they leave him likewise, and in his mind they are thoughts, which are thus cast into the thought-atmosphere of the

OLD AGE, DISEASE, AND DEATH

world. Furthermore, each thought is an entity, because obviously it could not exist for a fraction of a second if it did not have an individuality of some kind inhering in it and composing its essence which holds it as an entity in individualized form.

These streams of emanations from the creative center which man is — from this focus of life which man is — pass into the invisible realms as thoughts; and into the physical, visible realms also as his physical emanations. But the invisible ones — the thoughts good, bad, indifferent, highly colored, almost colorless, highly emotional, cold, hot, clean, sweet, infamous, all kinds of energies — leave the focus of life which man is; and it is these life-atoms, leaving man, which begin to evolve thenceforth on their own account, and in time become the intermediate nature of animals as they so evolve.

Man's emanations thus build up the animal world; the animals feed on these life-atoms of many kinds, physical, vital, astral, mental, and whatnot. As man thus emanates streams of life-atoms, so does the sun pour forth its vital essence in space, giving life and energy and ethereal substance to all that its invigorating rays touch, as well as its own atoms, its electrons, and whatnot, belonging to the physical sphere.

Thus does man continually pour forth his vitality. These life-streams issuing from him give life and evolutionary impulse and characteristics to the entities of the kingdoms below the human, because these subhuman kingdoms are the evolved productions of the thoughts and vital emanations of the human race.

Man's thoughts of hate and antagonism, his often beastly passions, and the various energies of an ignoble type which flow forth from him, are the roots of the things and entities in the subhuman kingdoms which man considers to be inimical and antagonistic to his own kingdom. On the other hand, human vital and mental emanations of a different type of aspirational, harmonious, kindly, amiable, symmetrical, character, act in a

OLD AGE, DISEASE, AND DEATH 53

similar way in providing the intermediate or psychical principles of the nonvenomous, harmless, and shapely beasts, as well as the large range of plants and flowers of beauty and usefulness in the vegetable kingdom.

Since nature is one vast organism, everything is connected with everything else. Therefore you cannot breathe, you cannot think, without setting in motion energies, forces, which ultimately will reach to the very uttermost limits of our home universe, and pass beyond those limits to the frontiers of other universes.

Therefore, even a thought about a star touches that star in due course of time, with infinitesimal effect, to be sure; but nevertheless this fact instances a wonderful truth. Furthermore it is a truth which makes one reflect.

Yes, the stars are perturbed even by your thought. And as regards those whose inner vision is more opened and who realize that the glorious luminaries scattered over the blue vault of night are but the physical garments of an inner and brilliant flame of consciousness, manifesting as the splendor of these cosmic suns — even as your consciousness manifests through you as a human being — as regards those who are thus beginning to be seers, their thought reaches the suns and the stars. Every one is a child of a sun, therefore an atom of spiritual energy; and what father does not know his child, and respond to its feeble cry?

What of death, the third of the woes that beset mankind? Death is the opener, the one giving vision; death is the greatest and loveliest change that the heart of nature has in store for us.

There is no death, if by that term we mean a perfect and complete, an utter and absolute, cessation of all that is. Death is change, even as birth through reincarnation, which is death to the soul, is change; there is no difference between death, so called, and life, so called, for they are one. The change is into another *phase of life*. Death is a phase

OLD AGE, DISEASE, AND DEATH 55

of life even as life is a phase of death. It is not something to be feared.

Man's physical body must sleep for a certain period in order to recuperate its forces, its powers; so must the psychical constitution of man have its rest time — in devachan.

Death is as natural, death is as simple, death itself is as painless, death itself is as beautiful, as the growth of a lovely flower. It is the portal through which the pilgrim enters the stage higher.

Exactly the same succession of events takes place in death that ensues when we lay ourselves in bed at night and drop off into that wonderland of consciousness we call sleep; and when we awaken rested, composed, refreshed, reinvigorated, and ready for the fray and problems of the daily life again, we find that we are the identic persons that we were before the sleep began. In sleep we have a break of consciousness; in death also there is a break of consciousness. In sleep we have dreams, or a greater or less unconsciousness; and in death we have dreams, blissful, wondrous, spiritual—or blank unconsciousness. As we awaken from sleep, so do we return to earth again in the next incarnation in order to take up the tasks of our karmic life in a new human body.

Here then is one difference between sleep and death, but a difference of circumstance and by no means of kind: after sleep we return to the same body; after death we take upon ourselves a new body. We incarnate, we reincarnate, every day when we wake from sleep; because what has passed, what has happened to us, what has ensued, while the physical body is asleep, is identic, but of very short term, with what takes place, with what ensues, when and after we die.

Death is an absolute sleep, a perfect sleep, a perfect rest; sleep is an incomplete death, an imperfect death, and often troubled with fevered and uneasy dreams on account of the imperfection of the conscious entity, call it soul, if you like, which the human ego is. Death and sleep are brothers. What happens in sleep takes place in death — but perfectly so. What happens in death and after death, takes place when we sleep — but imperfectly so. We incarnate anew every time when we awake, because awaking means that the entity which temporarily has left the body during sleep — the brain-mind, the astral-physical consciousness — returns into that body, incarnates itself anew, and thus the body awakens with the psychical fire again invigorating the blood and the tissues and the nerves.

In going to your bed and in lying down and in losing consciousness, have you ever feared? No. It is so natural; it is so happy an occurrence; it is so restful. Nature rests and the tired brain reposes; and the inner constitution, the soul, if you like so to call it, is temporarily withdrawn during the sleeping period into the higher consciousness of the human being — the ray, so to speak, is absorbed back into the inner spiritual sun.

Just exactly the same thing takes place at death, but in death the worn-out garment is cast aside; the repose also is long, utterly

OLD AGE, DISEASE, AND DEATH

beautiful, utterly blissful, filled with glorious and magnificent dreams, and with hopes unrealized which now are realized in the consciousness of the spiritual being. This dreaming condition is a panorama of the fulfillment of all our noblest hopes and of all our dreams of unrealized spiritual yearnings. It is a fulfillment of them all in glory and bliss and perfect completion and plenitude.

Death is an absolute sleep, a perfect sleep. Sleep is an imperfect, an incomplete, death. Hence, what happens when you sleep in that short period of time, is repeated perfectly and completely and on a grand scale when you die. As you awaken in the morning in the same physical body, because sleep is not complete enough to break the silver chain of vitality uniting the inner, absent entity with the sleeping body, just so do you return to earth after your devachanic experience, or experience in the heaven-world, the world of rest, of absolute peace, of absolute, blissful repose.

During sleep, the silver chain of vitality

OLD AGE, DISEASE, AND DEATH

still links the peregrinating entity to the body that it has left, so that it returns to that body along this psychomagnetic chain of communication; but when death comes, that silver cord of vitality is snapped, quick as a flash of lightning (nature is very merciful in this case), and the peregrinating entity returns to its cast-off body no more. This complete departure of the inner consciousness means the snapping of that silver cord of vitality; and the body then is cast aside as a garment that is worn out and useless. Otherwise, the experience of the peregrinating consciousness, the peregrinating entity or soul, is exactly the same as what happened to it during sleep, but it is now on a cosmic scale. The consciousness passes, and before it returns to earth again as a reincarnating ego it goes from sphere to sphere, from realm to realm, from mansion to mansion, following the wording of the Christian scriptures, which are in the Father's house.

Nevertheless, in a sense it is also resting, in utter bliss, in utter peace; and during this resting time it digests and assimilates the experiences of the last life and builds these experiences into its being as character, just as during sleep the resting body digests and assimilates the food it has taken in during the daytime, and throws off the wastes, and builds up the tissues anew; and when the reawakening comes it is refreshed. So is the reincarnating ego refreshed when it returns to earth.

Similarly with sleep: sleep is caused by the withdrawal from the physical body of the entity which filled it with its flame and gave it active life. That is sleep. And when that withdrawal of the inner entity is complete, the sleep as sleep is relatively perfect and there is relatively perfect unconsciousness — the sweetest sleep of all. For then the body is undisturbed, rests peacefully and quietly, rebuilds in its system what was torn down during the hours of active work or play.

If the withdrawal of the inner entity is incomplete or partial, then dreams occur, for the inner entity feels the attraction of the physical part of itself; the psychical man still feels that physical man working on it psychomagnetically, as it were; and the unconsciousness of sleep is disturbed by the vibrations of the physical man, of the animate body. This produces evil dreams, bad dreams, fevered dreams, strange dreams, unhappy dreams. If the withdrawal is somewhat more complete than in this last case, but not yet wholly complete, then there are happy dreams, dreams of peace.

When the sleep is what is called utterly unconscious sleep, it is so because the inner entity is the least affected by the psychomagnetic vibrations of the body and of the brain in particular. It itself, this consciousness or mind, is in a doze, resting, but with a certain amount of its consciousness remaining, which the brain, however, cannot register as a dream, because the separation between the body and the consciousness which has left it is too complete. But while this consciousness is thus half-awake, so to speak, half-resting, it is in that particular world, invisible to human eyes, to which its feelings and thoughts in the previous moments and hours have directed it. It is there as a visitant, perfectly well protected, perfectly guarded, and nothing will or can in all probability harm it — unless, indeed, the man's essential nature is so corrupted that the shield of spirituality ordinarily flowing around this inner entity is worn so thin that antagonistic influences may penetrate to it.

Rebirth, the awakening from the rest between earth lives, is the result of destiny, the destiny that you have made for yourself in past lives. You have builded yourself to come back here to earth; and that is why you are here now, because in other lives you builded yourself to reincarnate. You are your own parents; you are your own children; because you are yourself. You are simply the result, as a character, as a human being, of what you builded yourself to be in the past; and your future destiny — effect of necessity following cause — will be the result, the karma, of what you are now building yourself to be.

OLD AGE, DISEASE, AND DEATH 63

Here are the secret causes of rebirth: men hunger for light and know not where to look for it. The instincts of men tell them the truth, but they know not how to interpret them. Their minds, their intellects, are distorted through the teachings brought to them by those who have sought for light in the material world alone. To seek for light — a noble occupation indeed! — but to search the material world alone for it proves the searchers to have lost the key to the grander *Within* of which the material universe is but the shell, the clothing, the garment, the body, the outer carapace.

This is one of the secret causes of rebirth, of the rebirth of the human soul; because man, being an essential part of the universe, one with its very heart, in his heart of hearts and indeed in all his being, must obey the cosmic law of reimbodiment: birth, then growth, then youth, then maturity, then expansion of faculty and power, then decay, then the coming of the great peace — sleep, rest; and then the coming forth anew into manifested existence. Even so do universes reimbody themselves. Even so does a celestial body reimbody itself — star, sun, planet. Each one is a body such as you are in the lowest part of yourself; each one is an inseparable portion of the boundless universe, as much as you are; each one springs forth from the womb of boundless space as its child, just as you do; and one universal cosmic law runs through and permeates all, so that what happens to one, great or small, advanced or unadvanced, evolved or unevolved, happens to everyone, to all.

You carve your own destiny; you make yourself what you are. What you are now is precisely what in past lives you have made yourself now to be; and what you will in the future be, you are now making yourself to become. You have will, and you exercise this will for your weal or for your woe, as you live your lives on earth and later in the invisible realms of the spaces of space. This is one more, and the second, of the secret causes of rebirth.

OLD AGE, DISEASE, AND DEATH 65

There is a third secret cause, and perhaps it is the most materially effectual; and this third cause resides in the bosom of each one of us. It is the thirst for material life, thirst for life on earth, hunger for the pastures and fields wherein once we wandered and which are familiar to us, which bring us back to earth again and again and again and again. It is this *trishnā*, this *tanhā*, this "thirst" to return to familiar scenes that brings us back to earth — more effectual as an individual cause, perhaps, than all else.

The excarnate entity after death and before the return to rebirth on earth goes whither its sum total of yearnings, emotions, aspirations, direct it to go. It is the same even in human life on earth. A man will do his best to follow that career towards which he yearns or aspires; and when we cast this physical body off as a garment that has outworn its usefulness, we are attracted to those inner spheres and planes which during the life on earth last lived we had yearnings towards, aspirations towards. That is also precisely why we come back to this earth to bodies of flesh. It is the same rule but working in the opposite direction. We had material yearnings, material hungers and thirsts, latent as seeds in our character after death; and they finally bring us back to earth.

After death, the nobler, brighter, purer, sweeter seeds of character, the fruitage, the consequence, of our yearnings for beauty and for harmony and for peace, carry us into the realms where harmony and beauty and peace abide. And these realms are spheres just as earth is, but far more ethereal and far more beautiful, for the veils of matter are thinner, the sheaths of material substance there are not so thick as here. The eye of the spirit sees more clearly. Death releases us from one world, and we pass through the portals of change into another world, precisely as the inverse takes place when the incarnating soul leaves the realms of finer ether to come down to our own grosser and material earth life into the heavy body of physical matter.

The inner worlds to the entity passing

through them, as it has passed through this world, are as real — more real in fact — than ours is, because it is nearer to them. They are more ethereal, and therefore are nearer to the ethereality of the eternal pilgrim passing through another stage on its everlasting journey towards perfection; and these changes take place one after another, before the next incarnation on the returning wheel of the cycle — the pilgrim passing from one sphere to another through the revolving centuries, ever going higher, to superior realms, until the topmost point of the cycle of that particular pilgrim's journey is reached.

Therefore, fear not at all. All is well, for the heart of you is the universe, and the core of the core of you is the heart of the universe. As our glorious daystar sends forth in all directions its streams of rays, so does this heart of the universe, which is everywhere because nowhere in particular, constantly radiate forth streams of rays; and these rays are the entities which fill the universe full.

The Inner God

III

The Inner God

MAN per se is an invisible entity. What we see of him in and through the body is merely the manifestation of the inner man, because man essentially is a spiritual energy — a spiritual, intellectual, and psychomaterial energy, the adjective depending upon the plane on which we choose to discern his actions, for indeed he may be said to exist on all planes, inner and outer.

Though man is an invisible entity, he needs a physical body in which to live and with which to work upon this physical plane. He is a pilgrim of eternity. He came forth from the invisible part of cosmic being in aeons so far bygone in the past that mankind, except the great sages and seers, has lost all count thereof. He came out of the womb of cosmic being as an unself-conscious god-spark, and after wandering aeon after aeon after aeon after aeon through all the various inner worlds, passing at different stages through our own material sphere, and out again into the inner worlds, he finally became man, a self-conscious entity; and here we are. Future aeons of time will bring forth even on this our earth, into a far more perfect manifestation than at present, the locked-up faculties and powers existent in every human being; and in those days of the far distant future man will walk the earth a god, and he will walk this earth communing with his fellow gods, for he will then have brought forth the godlike powers now unevolved but nevertheless within his essence.

The heart of the heart of a human being is a god, a cosmic spirit, a spark of the central cosmic fire; and all evolution — which means unfolding what is within, unwrapping what is within the evolving entity, bringing forth what is locked up within — all evolution is merely bringing forth ever more into a more perfect manifestation the infolded, inlocked, wrapped up, energies, faculties, powers, organs, of the evolving entity. And with equal step, as these faculties and energies become more able to manifest themselves, become more perfectly evolved forth, does the organism through which they work — the body — show the effects of this inner evolving fire, of this energy within; and thus also the body itself so evolves, because automatically reflecting in itself each inner step taken forwards.

Human beings essentially are kin to the gods, kin to the cosmic spirits. The universe is our home. We cannot ever leave it. We are its children, its offspring, and therefore all that there is of boundless space is we ourselves in our inmost. We are native there, and boundless space is our home, and our instinct tells us therefore that "all is well."

Out of the invisible into the visible, like the growth of a plant, comes man, the man-plant of eternity. Beginning in one life on earth as a human seed, man grows to maturity, and produces or evolves forth what is locked up within; and then, with the natural decay of power, sinking to earth the body dies; and after a long period of rest and assimilation of experience in the invisible worlds, the inner spiritual flame comes again to earth for a new incarnation here.

Such in brief is the history of man, the man-plant of the ages. He is born and flowers a while and then dies down and rests, and with the returning life-season he springs anew into existence and again flowers and again dies down; but always the golden thread of self — the *sūtrātman* — passes through both time and space.

The spirit of man works through the human soul, and this human soul works through the vital-astral or ethereal vehicle or body or carrier: the transmitter of the energies or powers of the soul, which is psychomagnetically connected with the organs of the physical body; and this vital-astral principle thus works through the physical body and is carried into all parts of our physical frame, very much as the electric current is carried not only in but also over and around the wire. The spirit enfolds and guards and produces the human soul from within its own womb of selfhood; the human soul similarly permeates and produces the vital astral vehicle; and this in its turn permeates and produces the physical body.

A human seed comes from the ethereal worlds and is the laya-center through which streams from and builds up from the interior worlds the body to be, cell by cell. This seed grows into the physical body and, as it grows, incarnation of the human energies takes place concordantly, coordinately, and progressively, until maturity is reached, and at that point you see the full-grown man and more or less fully incarnated human soul.

Man is a complex and compound entity. His constitution ranges from body to spirit with all intermediate degrees of ethereal substances and energies and powers: seven in number. When these seven different degrees or grades are cooperating in vital activity then you have a complete man, a fully living man.

The human soul is neither immortal nor mortal per se; it is the seat of will, consciousness, intelligence, and feeling in the average human being. It is not immortal because it is not pure enough to be truly impersonal; if it were, it would not be human but superhuman. It is not wholly mortal, because its instincts, its movements, the operations of itself, are in a sense above purely mortal things of matter.

Man has holy loves, aspirations, hope, and vision. These belong to the spirit, which is immortal and deathless, and are transmitted through this intermediate nature or human soul, which human beings ordinarily call "I," much as the sunlight streams through the pane of glass in the window. The pane of glass is the vehicle or carrier or bearer or transmitter of this wondrous quality or force streaming from the sun above. The human soul is like this pane of glass, letting through as much of the spirit, of the golden sunlight of the spirit, as its evolutionary development enables it to do.

The human soul is conditionally immortal, if man allies himself by will and vision with the deathless spirit within and above; and mortal if he allows himself to be dragged down into what is called matter and material instincts and impulses, which are wholly mortal and which all die when death comes and frees the immortal spirit within; so that when man goes to his sublime home for the inter-life period of rest and peace, only bliss and high vision and a memory of all that is great and grand in our past life remain. The soul is itself an ethereal vehicle or carrier of the deathless and immortal energies of the productive spirit or monad.

The spirit is the immortal part of the human constitution. It is the monad, the monadic essence, that which tastes never of death, which lasts from the beginning of the manvantara to the end of that majestic period of cosmic manifestation; that which passes over the cosmic pralaya to begin its spiritual and other activities again when the new cosmic manvantara begins.

And so on in cyclical periods recurring forever, the spirit or monad is constantly growing: it is evolving, on its way to become the superspiritual, finally to become the divine, then the superdivine. Is that the end of its evolutionary possibilities? No, it advances ever, endlessly evolving and growing. But words fail here to describe this sublime conception. We cannot describe it in faltering human language. Our imagination falls palsied in any such attempt, and we can merely point to the evolutionary path vanishing in both directions into infinity and into eternity, as beginningless as it is unending.

That is the spirit or the monadic essence. It is the god within; it is the bright intelligence which stirs and moves the inmost articulations of the higher parts of the constitution, which movements, in their turn, are reflected in the brain-mind, in the human mentality. It is the source of everything that is great and noble and high, pure, good, aspiring, and clean, in the human being. It is the source of immortal love, the source

THE INNER GOD 79

of self-sacrifice, the source of all harmony and beauty, in the human being — the feeling of "I am." That is the spirit, the immortal monad, the undying, the stainless, the eternal inner god.

The human soul is a ray of it; this ray is what you recognize as the human being, the feeling that "I am I." And the soul, even as is the spirit, is a growing, advancing, progressing, evolving thing, growing ever greater; and in the far distant aeons of the future the soul will in its turn have so evolved forth its own innate and latent capacities, powers, and faculties — the splendor within itself — that from soul it shall have become spirit, *because the root or seed of the soul is a spiritual ray.* When this shall be in its culmination, then man shall have evolved from manhood into human godhood, from a human being into an incarnate god. Then will the god within you manifest itself with its transcendent faculties and powers and you will have become a living Buddha.

A human spirit is a deathless entity; it

is a part of the very fabric of the life universal in its inmost parts; and this spirit of man, this inner being, this spiritual soul, is pursuing an eternal pilgrimage in space, infinite in space and eternal in time. It passes from mansion to mansion of life, sojourning now here, now there, learning everywhere. The earth is one such mansion, in fact. Every sphere, every orb, in the celestial spaces, is another mansion of life.

The greatest lessons are learned in the invisible worlds; for this physical world that we see, despite its physical splendor, its illusory and magical interest, is but the shell, the garment, the body, the exterior; and just as from the interior of man flow forth all his thoughts, all his inspiration, all his genius, all his powers and energies, into the physical, and express themselves in the works that man does, so precisely all the manifestations that we see in the physical universe are but the expressions of the indwelling energies and faculties and powers and forces within that universe.

This eternal pilgrimage of the spiritual

THE INNER GOD 81

soul of man is not only in this cross section of the physical universe which our imperfect eyes can see, but most especially in the invisible realms, in what men call the spiritual worlds; for there are grades upon grades upon grades of them, higher and higher and higher and higher.

But this god within, an eternal pilgrim, learns eternally, going higher and higher and higher; and like human races on earth which, after reaching their culmination of splendor in civilizations, fall to rise again, so does the monad, the god, the spiritual soul, pass from the spiritual worlds down into ethereal matter, learning in each, and rising again out of each in order to reach a still higher peak of destiny; then down into the ethereal material realms again; then another rise to something still more lofty and sublime — and so on forever.

Oh, the peace and happiness that come from allying yourself with this inner splendor! This alliance of life and consciousness with this inner divinity brings everything of worth into your life, and in so allying yourself you become one with the energies and forces that control the universe, of which this inner god of you is a spark of the central fire; and when this inner union is achieved in fullness, you are on the pathway to human divinity. Buddhahood lies ahead of you.

This knowing of your inner self, of your inner god, is an expansion of your own consciousness; it is growth; it is evolution; it is coming to an understanding of all that exists. And when you have even some adumbration of this vision — some inkling of it, some hint of it — then such a thing as fear vanishes. Death loses all its terrors; for you know that you are one with the All, inseparable; that you are in fact that All itself; and therefore you are in your utmost reaches frontierless, because in very truth there are no utmost reaches. You never can reach the frontiers of yourself, your divine self, never; for the innermost parts of you are the very spiritual universe in which you live and move and have your being.

THE INNER GOD

It is the outer senses that distract our attention from the splendor within. In very truth, the five senses distract our attention away from the temple of the Most High, from the spirit within the human constitution manifesting through the human body. They are expressions of five different energies of the intermediate nature of man; and are the avenues — or function as such — by which man may become self-consciously aware of the outer world. In a way these senses are a help; and in another manner they are a detriment to progress. They are a help because they show somewhat of the nature that is around man, and it is through the senses that much of his ordinary consciousness at the present time functions, thus learning much about the world and fellow human beings. This learning ultimately teaches lessons of self-control and helps to awaken the faculties of pity, of love, of compassion, and of the will to do better, which are within man.

Man's inner spirit is the temple of infinitude, of its manifold life-energies and life-powers; and in the course of our cyclic progression into matter, these life-energies and life-powers manifest themselves outwardly. But we are now on the ascending arc of progressive development, and the whole trend of future evolution will be the development in mankind of the urge towards, and therefore the ultimate faculty of, looking inwards, so that individual man may know himself: know himself as one of the collaborators with the gods in the construction and government of the universe, as one of the sparks of the infinite, cosmic fire. For man has everything locked up within him — every power and energy that exists in the infinite spaces; and all evolution is but the bringing out of these locked-up powers, the unfolding as a flower unfolds, of what is within.

The inner god is forever within you, surrounding you, overshadowing you, waiting for you, waiting, waiting, waiting; brought out into manifestation only through the aeons, as the aeons pass by into the ocean of the past, through self-directed evolution, which

THE INNER GOD 85

is the development of the inner man — of what you are in the core of the core of your being — into manifestation through the outer man. The whole purpose of evolution is the thinning of the thick veils of mind and matter, so that the light in the holy temple which is the human heart may splendorously illumine man.

What prevents the light from illumining man and what is it that inhibits the action of the inner god? It is personality — that is all, and all the evils that flow forth from personality. Not individuality, which is godhood, the indivisible part of us, deathless and immortal, which tastes never of death or of decay — but personality: the small, mean, petty, restricted, limited things which form a close and compact atmosphere around our being, and which scarcely anything except immortal love can ever penetrate.

Personality, selfishness, egoism — these are the things which inhibit the manifestation of the divine energies within us. These it is which cripple men, so that men do not give full expression even to the powers and faculties that they now have.

The way by which to grow is to shed the personal in order to become impersonal; to shed, to cast aside, the limited in order to expand. How can the chick leave the egg without breaking its shell? How can the inner man expand without breaking the shell of the lower selfhood? How can the god within manifest itself — your own divine consciousness — until the imperfect, the small, the constricted, the personal in other words, has been surpassed, overpassed, left behind, abandoned, cast aside? It is in impersonality that lies immortality; in personality lies death. Therefore expand, grow, evolve, become what you are within! The gods call to us constantly — not in human words, but in those soundless symbols transmitted to us along the inner ethers which man's heart and soul interpret as spiritual instinct, aspiration, love, self-forgetfulness; and the whole import of what these voiceless messages are, is: "Come up higher!"

THE INNER GOD

What bliss it is to recognize one's kinship with all that is; to feel and to understand, and in feeling and in understanding thereby to act in accordance with the realization that one is akin to the gods who guide and control the boundless universe! And you can confabulate with the gods, if you first learn to confabulate with the god within.

Each human being is but the outermost expression of a divine entity, of an inner god, of a spiritual-divine being of which the human expression is an imperfect and feeble reflection — a faint and imperfect reproduction in human form of the spiritual powers within. So many men on earth, so many gods in the inner worlds.

When a man has become cognizant of the god within, has set this god free, so to speak, by giving up the petty personality of ordinary life — the man's own personal selfhood — and thus has broken the bonds fettering and binding the transcendent powers of the god within, then the messiah, the risen Christ, the savior of each one, can manifest its sublime faculties and powers. Then man shall be a living Christ — risen from the tomb of the lower selfhood into the atmosphere of spiritual glory; and the Christ light shall be working in him. He shall have awakened the living Buddha in his being, or rather, shall have evolved forth the Buddhic splendor already in his soul.

This divine being at the heart of each one is trying all the time to express itself better and ever better through the emotional and mental intermediate nature — through that which is called the human soul. This inner divinity is the source, the fountain, the origin, of all things that make men truly men; that make men great and grand and noble; that give men understanding, knowledge, compassion, love, and peace.

Commune in the silence with your inner god — that living inner chamber-temple within you, wherein, if you listen carefully, you can hear the whisperings of divinity, of the divinity which fills that chamber full. There lie truth and wisdom and understanding and ineffable peace. Open the portals of your human selfhood to the rays from the divine sun within; enter into this chamber in your heart of hearts; become one with your self, your divine self, the god within you; *be* the god which you are in the core of the core of your being!

The Great Heresy of Separateness

IV

The Great Heresy of Separateness

A CONCENTRATION of thought upon the personal individual, seeking personal rather than spiritual freedom, is the way which leads downward. The pathway of self is the pathway to ever deeper realms and spheres of matter, until finally annihilation comes at the end of the cosmic cycle, when matter itself dissolves: māyā, as matter, is illusion.

Aspire; cultivate your higher faculties. Beware of the glamorous lights of the lower nature, and particularly of the lower intermediate nature which is called the psychical. There is nothing so deceptive as the false lights of māyā. Often fine-looking flowers contain deadly poison either in bud or in thorn or in both. The honey thereof is death-dealing, bringing death to the human soul. Seek first your own spiritual and intellectual powers; bathe in the light of your own spiritual nature so that you shall have vision and will power; and then these other faculties will grow in you naturally, evenly, properly, easily.

The law of laws of the universe is self-forgetfulness, not concentration of attention upon one's personal freedom, not even upon your individuality. The primal law of the universe is living unto all things, not the doctrine that each must live for himself in order to develop for himself the spiritual powers within. The latter is true enough as a bald and imperfect statement; but it is also misleading, dangerous, unwise, and therefore unholy as a statement of esoteric training, unless properly qualified — always qualified with the accompanying doctrine: Give up thy life if thou wouldst find it. Live to benefit mankind, for this is the first step. If you will have the sun, then leave the earth and its clouds.

The great heresy and the only real heresy is the idea that anything is separate, distinct,

THE HERESY OF SEPARATENESS 95

and different essentially, from other things. That is a wandering from natural fact and law, for nature is nothing but coordination, cooperation, mutual helpfulness; and the rule of fundamental unity is perfectly universal: everything in the universe lives for everything else.

It is this sense of separateness that is the cause and root of all evil. It brings forth the craving for *me: I want, I am, mine.* And it is the sense of personal separateness, imagining that one is utterly separate from all others, utterly different, that prevents one from becoming that inner god within. For by becoming that inner god you become consciously at one with the universe of which you are a child, an inseparable part; and that means drawing upon strength inexhaustible, wisdom without compass, drinking at the fountains of inspiration which flow from the heart of the universe. Every one is rooted in the common fountain of the cosmic life-intelligence-substance.

Selfishness is restrictive; it is the founda-

96 THE HERESY OF SEPARATENESS

tion of all degeneration, of all moral decay, of all mental and physical weakness; it is crippling; it binds you in, and leaves you no room to expand and to grow. Selfishness is the root of all evil, and therefore of weakness of mind, of lack of faculty, of lack of power, of lack of judgment, of lack of discrimination, of lack of a feeling heart. Selfishness is therefore the fertile cause of all misfortune and pain. Everything that cripples the native faculties of the human constitution arises out of selfishness. It brings about a deplorable and evil-working view restricted to your own little circle of thought. You are then a prisoner, imprisoned in your own selfishness, and therefore are you fearfully crippled in life's noblest battles. Selfishness makes you a prisoner — and your prison is your lower self.

Oh, the feeling of freedom, of true manhood, when one leaves the prison of the lower selfhood and feels one's oneness with the All; for in very truth you are that All in the mystic arcana of your own inmost being.

It is selfishness and ignorance that cause

THE HERESY OF SEPARATENESS

men to differ and quarrel among themselves; for in self-seeking, men use the forces of nature for personal and selfish ends — sometimes deliberately, sometimes half-consciously. This is done by our free will, which is in itself, nevertheless, a divine power or quality.

We have wills; they are free. We are part of the energies of the universe, for we are inseparable from it. We use our wills sometimes aright and sometimes awry; and when we use them aright we see the wondrous mysteries in the hearts and faces of our fellows and recognize greatness in their innermost being; for greatness is also in us, and greatness always recognizes greatness. And when we use these forces wrongly, unrightly, or awry, we employ the colorless forces of the universe, but do it evilly, seeking profit for self. Having free wills we use these energies; and we do it in ignorance of the law — the law of nature.

Ignorance is a bane to man. If we knew what we were doing; if we knew that we were throwing into disarray the forces of the universe, arousing evil passions in ourselves and in other men; if we could but realize this fundamental truth of nature — that all things have a common root in ceaseless peace and harmony — no sane man would then tolerate discord and evil in himself but would work to enlighten and aid his brothers.

Ignorance is the greatest foe of man. And the fruits of ignorance are unhappiness, sorrow, pain, disease, and suffering.

Selfishness is ignoble. It is also very unwise, because there is nothing like selfishness to cripple you and to mire your feet in the slough of the lower selfhood. The road to success is the quenching of personality, the becoming impersonal, so that your feet are not mired by the mud, by the clinging dirt, of material existence. The law is the same for all: be impersonal, be self-forgetful!

A man who thinks of naught but self, *me, my* plans, *my* property, *my* wishes, *my* thoughts, makes a perfect cocoon of imperfect and ugly selfhood around himself,

THE HERESY OF SEPARATENESS

through which nothing can shine, and which is like an adamantine wall around him more hard and durable than steel.

Indeed, we are surrounded by barriers of our own making, of our own construction, of our own thought-fabric, and our worst barriers are within us. As man's consciousness grows, it bursts the bonds hemming it in, breaks down the barriers preventing its expression, and the inner splendor shines forth.

Rigidity of thought, rigidity of opinions, are barriers to true spiritual progress, because they signify dogmatism, they signify the blinds of self-satisfaction. They actually mean, to change the metaphor, the closing of the doors of the mind to the entrance of a new truth, because men are never rigid and inelastic, so to say, in their souls — they are never rigid and inelastic in their minds — *unless they are self-satisfied;* and there is nothing that blinds one's inner vision so greatly to truth as does self-satisfaction. Remember also that most human beings are

100 THE HERESY OF SEPARATENESS

self-satisfied for a little while, but not for long.

On the contrary, an open mind, an eager intellect, the desire to have an unveiled spiritual perception, a readiness to receive truth and to give it to others from the full-flowing sympathy of one's own heart — all these insure true spiritual progress and are thus the answering signs of some advancement along the pathway of spiritual evolution.

Avoid, therefore, rigidity. Let your mind be open; let your intellect be eager to seize any new aspect of truth that may present itself to you. An unveiled spiritual perception is merely the loss of personality in opinions, in views, and of self-satisfaction. Seeing the impersonal: that is having an unveiled spiritual perception.

The main thing that closes the doors against the entrance of light is the feeling that may be expressed in the words: "I have all that I need to know." Egoism! This feeling arises out of pure egoism. The opposite of egoism is impersonal vision of spiritual truths

THE HERESY OF SEPARATENESS 101

working in your soul and thus molding it to receive impersonal, universal impressions.

Anything will aid you in your spiritual growth that will take you away from your animal-self, that will cause you to forget your personal being and take you out into the great breadth of nature and give you thoughts of compassionate, impersonal service. What comfort, what hope, what solace, what peace, in forgetting oneself!

Anything that takes you away from yourself with its small circle of personal limitations, of selfish ideas and idiosyncrasies, egoistic thoughts and emotions, into impersonal service, into tending something, mothering something if you like, in self-forgetful work for others, greatly helps you spiritually. Tending a tree, tending a flower, looking after the interests of some human being, busy with your book, with your writing, with your machine, with your tools, whatever it may be — anything that will cause you to forget the personal self — helps you in spiritual growth, self-forgetfulness. What reward comes to the

102 THE HERESY OF SEPARATENESS

man or woman who does this! That is the secret of the call of the religions. It enables a man or a woman to forget the lower personal self. And you can achieve exactly the same results by giving full field to the spiritual powers within your breast in any kind of impersonal work.

Sweet are the fruits of self-forgetfulness — the complete oblivion of your personality in something so beautiful and impersonal that human tongue cannot describe it! For self-forgetfulness, pity, compassion, and peace are the fruits of the cosmic harmony, which is the very heart of the universe. When you begin to realize this fact, then within your soul there begins the growth of something which is indescriptible, which cannot be expressed in words, but which is at once light, and life, and peace, and wisdom, and almighty love — impersonal, universal; so that everything that is, everywhere, has a fascination for you, for you love it.

And yet the whole exterior universe is but the garment or shadow of something invisi-

THE HERESY OF SEPARATENESS

ble, of the inner life, of which each human being, and indeed every entity, is an inseparable part; for all entities and things are rooted in this inner life, and therefore whatever any one of us may do reacts with corresponding force upon all other entities and things.

Each one is his brother's keeper, being as we are inseparably bound together by unbreakable bonds of origin and of destiny. Fundamentally we are all one. Every son of man is the keeper of his brothers, in the sense that he acts upon them, and their minds and hearts react against what he says to them. And his responsibility becomes consciously, self-consciously, the heavier just in proportion as his own evolution is the more advanced.

We make ourselves to be exactly what we are; and we are, at the same time, our brothers' keepers, because each one of us, *each one of us,* is responsible for an aeonic chain of causation. There is law in this universe; things are not ruled by chance; and a man cannot think or speak or act without affecting other beings, to their weal or to their woe.

Sow an act, and you will reap a habit. Sow a habit, and you will reap a destiny, because habits build character. This is the sequence: an act, a habit, a character, and a destiny. You are the creator of yourself. What you make yourself to be now, you will be in the future. What you are now, is precisely what you have made yourself to be in the past. What you sow, you shall reap.

If you sow for yourself, for purely selfish ends only, you will reap accordingly. The man who has such small love for the intrinsic beauty of right action as to say to himself: I am going to be good merely in order that I shall get something, a better fortune, a better future, a better body, has his good sowing already spoiled with a whole handful of tares — his selfish desire. There is nothing so belittling as personality, nothing will so diminish your soul in its strength as concentration on your own selfish personal affairs and a forgetting of the welfare of others.

THE HERESY OF SEPARATENESS

The man who thinks of others before himself is already great. The man who gives up his life that others may live is already great. The man who forgets himself in impersonal service to humanity is the greatest of all; and such a man reaps a destiny — because he has builded a corresponding character — which is godlike.

Nature demands of all human beings co-operation, brotherhood, kindly feeling, love, self-forgetfulness, working for others. The selfish man or woman always, sooner or later, goes to the wall. The wicked may flourish like the green bay tree for a little while, but not for long. Selfishness is shriveling; it means cold; it means the opposite of the expansive, warm power of love.

Nature will not tolerate for long persistent self-preferment to the detriment of others: for the very heart of nature is harmony, the very fabric and structure of the universe is coordination and cooperation, spiritual union; and the human being who seeks self-preferment unremittingly, without surcease, ends in that far-distant country of the "mystic West," the land of forgotten hopes, the land of spiritual decay; for nature will have none of him for long. He has set his puny, undeveloped will against the mighty currents of the cosmos, and sooner or later he is washed on to some sandbank of the river of life, where he decays. Nature will not tolerate persistent and inveterate selfishness.

Look at a tree. Look at our bodies. Each is builded up of hosts of minor things, of minor entities, all working together, and composing one thing, in which they all live and move and have their being, and therein they partake of the common life.

When a man acts harmoniously, he acts in accordance with the universal scheme and law; and harmony in consciousness and thought and therefore in action is what men understand by the term ethics. Ethics are not a convention; morals are not a convention; they are rooted in the harmony, in the central laws, of being; they are based on the very structural harmony of the universe.

THE HERESY OF SEPARATENESS 107

This instinct of ethics thus springs from within your inner constitution. It comes forth from your spiritual being recognizing harmony, order, the stateliness and majesty of beauty — beauty in thought, beauty in aspiration and feeling, beauty in action.

Knowledge is of loving deeds the child — this is one of the sublimest truths. Of the mysteries, of the higher mysteries, you cannot have knowledge unless your heart is filled with love, and overflowing with it; and knowledge comes from the exercise of the spiritual powers within you. This exercise is most easily achieved in doing deeds of loving kindness, in feeling and practicing brotherhood, in helping and sharing with others, in helping others and sharing with them the blessings that you have.

How noble it is, how grand it is, for men to feel their common kinship with each other, to feel almighty love stirring in the heart, to sense the feeling of our common brotherhood, and to live to benefit mankind!

Love is the Cement of the Universe

V

Love is the Cement of the Universe

LOVE shows the way and lights the path; love is the flowing forth of the permeant light, the Buddhic splendor, the Christ light, at the heart of the universe — that love which, working in gods and men, teaches us to know beauty when we see it, especially inner beauty, to recognize greatness and splendor in others, from knowing the greatness and splendor in our own inmost being.

Love is the cement of the universe; it holds all things in place and in eternal keeping; its very nature is celestial peace, its very characteristic is cosmic harmony, permeating all things, boundless, deathless, infinite, eternal. It is everywhere, and is the very heart of the heart of all that is.

Love is the most beauteous, the holiest,

thing known to human beings. It gives to man hope; it holds his heart in aspiration; it stimulates the noblest qualities of the human being, such as the sacrifice of self for others; it brings about self-forgetfulness; it brings also peace and joy that know no bounds. It is the noblest thing in the universe.

"Love ye one another" — a beautiful saying this, for it is an appeal to the very core of your nature, to the divine within you, to the inner god, whose essence is a celestial splendor. The essential light of you is almighty love.

Love is protective; love is puissant; it is all-penetrating; and the more impersonal it is, the higher it is and the more powerful. It knows no barriers either of space or of time, for it is nature's fundamental activity, nature's fundamental law, and it is the universal bond of union among all things. It will not only eat away the obstinacy of the stoniest of human hearts and dissolve the substance of the most adamantine of human minds, but it will slowly infuse its life-giving warmth everywhere. Nothing can bar its passage, for it is the very life-essence of the universe. For all beings and things are one, ultimately, all rooted in the one LIFE, and through all flows the steady, uninterrupted current of almighty love.

Love is the great attractive power which links thing to thing, human heart to human heart; and the higher one goes in evolution, the closer does love enwrap its tendrils through all the fiber of one's being; or, to change the figure of speech, the more does the human heart expand with love, until finally it embraces in its folds all the universe, so that one comes to love all things both great and small, without distinction of place or time. Oh, the blessedness of this feeling, of this realization! It is divine; for love, impersonal love, is divine.

Personal love is but a reflection of it; and personal love is fallible, because the ray is so feeble. Anything that has as its motivating cause the desire for personal benefit is not true love.

In personal love the veils of personality begin to thicken before the inner eye, because personal desire collects and thickens into one's aura — the surrounding psychic atmosphere — and condenses it, and this it is which causes the thickening of the psychic veils, obscuring the inner vision and understanding. The essence of true love is self-forgetfulness, and to this rule there are no exceptions.

If a man's heart and mind are filled solely with a personal love, then he loves this but he does not love that; he loves something over there, but he does not love some other thing here, or vice versa — in other words, his love is limited in direct ratio with its personal character. That is the kind of love that is not wholly true, that is limited.

Impersonal love is lovely, beautiful, and has no trace of the things that we all dislike. It is always kindly to everything and to everybody — to beings and things both great and small; it is intuitive.

Responsibility, trust, confidence, love — these indeed bring happiness, strength, and joy. But you will not understand these grand qualities nor truly feel them if your heart is filled with purely personal limited feelings and thoughts. Your heart will not have a place for them, will not contain them if it is filled with merely personal things.

For personal love is never responsible, has no sense of responsibility. It cannot trust; it cannot truly confide; it cannot utterly give, because the "I" is there in strength all the time and its one thought is: for me, for me, *for me*. This is the trouble in the world today, and all troubles and sorrows will cease in large, large, *large* degree when men and women can love each other impersonally, when men can look upon their fellow man as a human hero, and when women will trust their own sex, which they will do when they have this vision — the vision sublime.

It is precisely this selfish personal love which has brought sorrow, suffering, and misery into human life, just as impersonal love cleanses and purifies and makes men's hearts glad.

There is something beautiful about a human heart which can give itself without thought of recompense or of the pain that the giving temporarily may cause the giver. That love which is given without thought of or for self, which has no frontiers and no conditions, is divine. True love is impersonal always.

Love is peace; love is harmony; love is self-forgetfulness; love is strength; it is power; it is vision; it is evolution. Its power so expands the inner nature that slowly you become sympathetic, because you become at one with the entire home universe in which you live and move and have your being; and because it is harmony itself, and because it is of the very essence of the core of the universe, you become at one with the divinity in the heart of all things.

Impersonal love is divine. It illuminates the heart; it broadens the mind; it fills the soul with a sense of oneness with all that is; so that you could no more injure a fellow creature than you could do a wrong deliberately and willfully to some thing, or to the individual, that personally you love best on earth.

Love is mighty. It is the greatest thing in human life, because it is the greatest thing in the life of the gods, of which human life is but a poor and inadequate reflection. One's whole nature pours out its glorious stream of sympathy for all that is. Life becomes ennobled from the very beginning, and you see before you, even on those distant horizons of the future, complete understanding of everything, with everything, and a reunion of all entities and things into one consciousness, wherein hatred, strife, disunion, misunderstanding, will have vanished away.

A faint reflection of this love is the love of one human being for another — very faint it is, but it is at least the beginning of self-forgetfulness. But once the soul is illuminated with impersonal love's holy splendor, then you truly live.

Impersonal love asks no reward, it gives all and therefore gives itself. Love is an illumination. Love is inspiring; it opens the doors of the mind, because it cracks the bonds of the lower selfhood hemming in the god within. When you love impersonally then the divine fires flow out, and man becomes truly man.

Love is a mighty power. Perfect love casteth out all fear. He whose heart is filled with love and pity never knows what fear is; there is no room for it in his heart. Love all that lives and you then ally yourself with invincible cosmic powers and you become strong and spiritually and intellectually clairvoyant. You will never fear anything in proportion as your heart is filled with love and understanding, because love — perfect love — bringeth understanding. You will then never fear poverty; you will never fear death.

You can overcome fear by visualizing to yourself actions and thoughts of high and noble courage. Think of yourself as doing courageous actions. Study and admire courageous actions in others. Study and admire courageous thought in others. Grow to love courage, so that you follow it. Then you become it and fear will vanish away like the mists of the night before the rising sun. There lies the secret of overcoming fear: it is to use the creative imagination.

These are practical rules of ethics, practical rules of human conduct; and oh, the pity that mankind has lost sight of them! Men will be ruled by fear just as long as they love themselves; for then they will be afraid of everything that is going to happen — afraid to venture, afraid to act, to do, to think, for fear lest they lose. And they will then lose. "That which I feared has come upon me!" It is always so.

It is the great men who do not fear, who venture, who act, who do — for they are the doers; and they are also the thinkers of the world; because in either case they have no fear. They love the things that they do. Therefore they have no fear.

The strong man is he who loves, not he who hates. The weak man hates because he is limited and small. He can neither see nor feel the other's pain and sorrow, nor even sense so easy a thing as the other's viewpoint. But the man who loves recognizes his kinship with all things. His whole nature shines with the beauty within him, expands with the inner fire which flames itself forth in beautiful and symmetrical thoughts, and therefore in beautiful and kindly acts. His very features will soften and become kindly; he will not be feared; he will not be hated.

Impersonal love is magical; it works marvels; it will break even stony human hearts. Nothing, not even hate, can withstand its passage. Follow the ancient law: hate not. Conquer hatred by love. Requite never hate with hate, for thus you but add fuel to an unholy flame. Requite hatred with compassion and justice. Give justice when you receive injustice. Thus you ally yourself with nature's own spiritual procedures and you become a child of the cosmic life, which thereafter will beat in your own heart with its undying pulses.

Be yourself, and expand your sympathies;

touch with the tendrils of your consciousness the hearts of other human beings. What delight to feel, as it were, the inner and electrical quiver that your own soul experiences when you have touched the heart of a fellow human being!

Let your heart expand with the divine energies latent within it: love, compassion, pity, understanding of others, kindliness, the vision of beauty in the light of love, and of love in the light of the beauty that itself emanates.

Be kindly; refuse to hate. Let your heart expand.

Another step which leads to the pathway of divine love is forgiveness. Forgiveness is the movement of the heart which will lead you to make the first step on the upward way; it is in truth one of the steps to divine love. True forgiveness requires strength of character, real manhood, real discrimination, and intellectual power; it is the refusing to bear resentment, to nourish a grudge, to cultivate hatred; and forgiveness means also to cleanse your own heart of these vile and degrading impulses.

Here is the illustration: you have been wronged. Which of these twain will you do: nourish resentment, cultivate hatred, bide the time when you may pay back in the same coin, thereby increasing the trouble and heart agony of the world by double? Or will you say: No, I will forgive; I myself have laid the way open for this, for I myself in the past have brought this pain upon me. Unhappy man who harms me! I will forgive him.

The evildoer knows not what he is doing. He is weak. He is blind. Whereas he with a forgiving heart sees and is strong: for love forgives all things, and the reason that it does so is because it sympathizes, it understands. Understanding brings insight.

Learn to forgive; and forgive when forgiving is needed. Not the mere lip-forgiving, when there is no temptation upon you to hate, but forgive when forgiveness means calling forth the strength in you. Love when there is a mean and selfish impulse upon you to hate, because loving then shows spiritual exercise which means strength and grandeur within you.

This is very strengthening for you in your inner constitution. The effort and the result pacify disputes, allay distress, stimulate trust and kindly feeling; and to him who sincerely and successfully forgives there come a peace and a consciousness of strength which nothing else ever can bring.

Forgive and love your fellows, and let that love which fills your heart with its holy light and illumines your mind with its divine splendor, let it go out to all that lives, without bounding it, without laying frontiers for it; and your reward will be very great. For love is not only evocative of love in other hearts, but it is very elevating to yourself. It brings out not solely the beautiful things in the souls of those whom you love, but it develops your own faculties and powers.

Forgive and love; and you thereby place your feet on the pathway which will lead you direct to the spiritual sun which rises eternally with healing in its wings. Forgive and love; and before you know it, you will feel the sweet influence of the Buddhic splendor — the Christ spirit — stealing all through your being. You will then become a beneficent power on earth, not merely beloved of your fellow men, but a blessing to all beings. You will then be making a beginning in the proper use of the sublime faculties and powers native to the god within you; you will understand all things, because love is truly clairvoyant and is a mighty power.

Learn to forgive, for it is sublime; learn to love, for it is divine.

The Chela Path

VI

The Chela Path

BEAUTIFUL indeed is the bond between teacher and disciple: the sense on the part of the disciple of utmost confidence and love, so that nothing, he feels, could be hid from his teacher's knowledge; and on the part of the teacher, the understanding, the compassion, the love, yea, sometimes and often indeed, commendation. If the disciple has gratitude towards his teacher, the teacher in a sense has gratitude towards his disciple, for he sees in him the growing life of a new Master of Compassion to flower forth in the aeons to come.

Be of good cheer! Follow the pathway upon which you have entered. Follow it faithfully despite the mistakes that you may make, and the stumbling blocks that you have to pass over. Follow that pathway leading ever more inward to the god within you: it will lead you to the very heart of the universe; and as you advance along this path, you will gain an accession of inner power, an increase of inner faculty, and a growth of the spiritual and intellectual portions of your constitution, which will be the opening to you of doors through which you may look with each new recurrence ever farther inward towards that heart of the universe.

Every initiation is but the opening of a new door of experience in the realms of the inner life. Each new door closes behind you forevermore. You never can pass backward; but while you find yourself in a new world for the time being, with added faculty, with increase of power, with new powers within you to exercise, nevertheless you will always see another door ahead of you. These "doors" are likewise called "veils," and as you pass one veil, there is always another veil beyond. Each new temple-chamber, veiled the one

THE CHELA PATH

from the other, contains a greater light than the last one entered.

Great indeed is the reward of those who succeed — ineffable, glorious; and that success is but the beginning of still greater successes to follow, for every step ahead opens up a new vista of possibilities in the endless and ever-changing panorama of the life of the universe. Every step forward is a going into a greater light, in comparison with which the light just left is shadow; but the holy light of truth and light and love shines through every veil, and that light liveth forever in you, for it is your essential self.

Becoming one with your essential self, passing veil after veil of obscuring, personal vehicles — whether those vehicles be physical or astral or psychological or mental, or even spiritual — going ever more and more inward or upward, you approach ever more and more near, ever closer to the inner god, which is the essential life of that truth; and hence when you become it, your consciousness from being merely human becomes the consciousness of the universe. The inner god of you is one of the spiritual building blocks of the boundless universe, and the boundless universe is a fabric, a web, of consciousness. Knowing yourself, you shall know all things.

The way of growth is not a difficult way. It is called a steep and thorny path, but it is so only to the selfish, acquisitive, passional, lower man. The way of the spirit is the way of light, it is the way of peace, it is the way of hope, it is the way to the sun. Set your feet firmly on this path; follow it and attain!

On this difficult path the aspirant is sustained by the love of his guide, but he must walk every step along the pathway to victory alone. He is not carried there. Every step he himself must take. In ordinary human existence we make our own way in the world, we feed ourselves, we inform ourselves, we train ourselves. If that is a necessity here, it is tenfold the same necessity in the esoteric life. There must we ourselves win everything, because we are simply bringing out

THE CHELA PATH 131

what is within us; our own will, our own consciousness, must become awakened, fully awakened, and by our own efforts.

You cannot see unless you use your own faculty of vision. You cannot understand by someone else's understanding. You must gain everything you ever have, in the esoteric training. You yourself must awaken in your own soul the holy flame; and it is the same with every other step in spiritual and intellectual progress that you make. You yourself must experience the unspeakable delight of compassion — the ineffable feeling of being at one with the All. You yourself must be the vehicle of the inner light, must gain it. It is both in you and above you, invigorating you and inspiring you.

Spiritual light comes to you from within; you do not receive light — the light of the spirit — from outside. All that the teacher can do is to help you to brush away the enshrouding veils of selfhood in many different manners and in diverse and divers ways. All spiritual illumination comes to you now, and ever will come to you, from the Master within yourself. There is no other possible pathway to the light. All growth is from within; all illumination is from within; all inspiration is from within; all initiation is from within.

Aspiration is real prayer; it is a constant raising of ourselves from day to day, trying each day to go a little higher towards the god within. This means harmony, inner harmony, peace. Therefore, having harmony and peace within you, in your mind, in your heart, that state of mind and heart will reflect itself in your physical body, and your body will function harmoniously, which means that it will function in health.

Moreover, an atmosphere of lofty conceptions and of kindly thoughts clarifies and refines the auric atmosphere around every human being, and it is the bounden duty of every disciple on the path to do just this. Aspirations towards high and noble things even refine the atoms of our entire constitution.

THE CHELA PATH 133

The disciple should have always in mind the consciousness of, the brooding thought about, these teachings. They should be held in your consciousness continually. There should be a brooding over them. They should go to bed with you and be with you when you arise, be with you when you are clothing yourself, or bathing yourself, or eating your meals, even when you do your duties. Have the mind brooding all the time on these wonderful doctrines. This "superconscious" mind is the root of you, the divine essence, on and in which this brooding consciousness dwells.

Such is meditation: taking a subject for thought and dwelling upon it in thought in an impersonal way, meanwhile searching within yourself for the answer, for more light upon it; and if this method of meditation be faithfully followed, finally light will come. Exercise makes it so easy, habit endows it with such attractiveness, that finally the time will come when you will be meditating all day long, even though your hands may be busy with your daily tasks. Inexpressible happiness and peace are in it.

One does not need to go into his private chamber and to sit or to stand or to lie, and with an effort of the will try to whip the brain to think of certain things. Concentration means centering your mind on a point of thought or object of thought and holding to it. It is easy to accomplish and the way to do it is to be interested in a thing. If you are really interested in a thing your mind automatically will concentrate itself upon it.

But the best form of meditation is the constant thought, yearning, aspiration, to be your best, to live your noblest, and to keep this thought with you day and night. If the yearning to be one's best and to live one's noblest is derivative from the spirit of compassion, welling up in the heart like a holy river of energy, it will lead one quickly to the Gates of Gold.

Yet, the next step on the path is taken when the disciple is ready: it all depends upon the disciple; the teacher can do nothing except to awake him; the disciple is the one to decide. For when the disciple is ready, the teacher is waiting.

There comes a time in human evolution when a man or a woman arrives at a point where he wants to concentrate all his energies — spiritual, intellectual, psychical, astral, vital, physical, everything — on one object, namely, to make himself a fit servant and servitor of his fellow human beings without any other distractions or calls of duty. This is called *chelaship:* the state of discipleship. But this path of discipleship is for the few.

Those who follow this pathway of spiritual progress and illumination — disciples of the esoteric life, living the chela life — have pledged themselves to give up self for the world, to have no personal property of their own, to give up life and all that there is, to the holiest cause they know. For these disciples of the life beautiful, nonresistance is right: they have sworn never to strike back; never to lift a hand in self-defense if the attack be on the chela alone; never to protect one's personal self against libel or slander, that is, if it be only for the protection of the individual's personality; to turn the other cheek when smitten; and give one's shirt also when the cloak is asked. But even these chelas are pledged to check wrong, to stay the pathway of evildoing, to stop it if possible, when the evildoing is directed against another; because an esotericist will do for another what he may never do for himself.

The chelas close their minds to pleasures as to pains: for the ideal man is one whose will is not swayed nor is his judgment biased either by pleasure or by pain. The superior man is one who stands firm and is not led astray by pleasure, nor does he weaken under pain.

The chelas give themselves to benefit the world; they give up all personal matters in order that they may live for the universe. These few give themselves; and more it is possible for no one to give. This is the path of the Buddhas and of the Christs.

Chelaship, or the training for Masterhood,

is a strenuous and heart-stirring work. Every step of it is joy, although at times there come psychological reactions which must be guarded against. The chela life may be likened to the man who is engaged upon some important, fascinating, most interesting, but very strenuous physical work. He labors, he tires, the breath comes quick and fast, the sweat bedews his brow, and bedews his body, but yet he feels growing under his hand, as it were, a work of marvelous beauty. He is inspired to give to it every ounce of strength that is in him. The chela knows that over the distant hills, perhaps for him, if his karma is favorable, not so far distant, there lies the temple of wisdom, and that its doors will open for him if he can reach it, and reach it clean and strong. If he reaches it with soiled feet, with feet which he has not washed with the tears of his eyes and the blood of his heart, he must retrace his steps, or wait until the time come when no longer will the heart bleed, and no longer will the eyes be blinded with the tears of selfish personal devotion to merely personal ends. Then the eyes will be lightened with the undying inner flame, and the heart will, as it were, beat only for others, because it will be utterly self-forgetful. Then beauty, then inexpressible joy, then unimaginable strength and peace, will enter into his life.

Chelaship in itself is not difficult. In itself it is easy, almost inexpressibly easy. It means giving up pain, giving up sorrow, giving up anger, giving up lust, giving up selfishness, giving up all the things that injure us and blind us and cripple us and retard us. It means being clean, sweet, fresh, strong, pure, beautiful. It means beginning to live the life of an incarnate god. It means becoming at one with one's inner god, ever more and more; a little at first, a little more at the next effort, and so forth, for at each effort the chela gains more and more of the inner light, of the inner life, of the inner inspiration — of the inner Buddhic splendor. In other words, it means becoming ever more and more at one with the inner Master. In every human being there is now, even now, an exalted entity, a Mahatma.

The life of chelaship is a beautiful life, and the first rule is: to live to benefit mankind. This is the first step in vision, the first step of spiritual growth, the first step of upward progress — not to live in order to benefit yourself, but to benefit the universe; which, indeed, and from another standpoint, is yourself, for it is you and you are it.

The chela life actually is the simplest thing in the world: to be kindly, to be gentle, to be just, and to cultivate your spiritual and intellectual powers. Do not be swept away ever by anger or passion. Not only do they not pay, but thereby you make bad karma which some day you will have to meet and overcome.

Be self-forgetful; be impersonal and therefore unattached to matter; be detached and therefore impersonal. Be great of heart and great of soul, and then you can attain by being impersonal. Bear injustice with equanimity, thereby you become magnanimous —

great of heart. Never strike back; never retaliate; be silent; be patient. Protect others; protect yourself not at all.

Forgive injuries. With a heart filled with love for all that is, and complete and perfect forgiveness of all injuries, past, present, and to come, the chela surrounds himself with a mighty protective power, for these spiritual energies purify the heart; they stimulate the intellect; they elevate the soul. Thus will your soul shine through your body like a lamp shining through glass, and you will illuminate not only those with whom you are, but by your peace, by your quiet, you will lighten and will light the pathway for them.

Be bold in your learning, but not overbold. Be courageous as you press forward on this old, old path of the ages, leading to the heart of the universe; but be not rash. Guard well your speech, lest something pass out unseen with the words: for you can never recall it. Dare, will, know, and be silent!

Let yourself grow naturally as the flower opens its petals, as the bud opens its heart.

THE CHELA PATH

Is there any reason or need why the eyes should be continuously blinded with tears, and why the feet should be continuously washed with the blood of the heart?

Do not be discouraged if you fail, if you do not live up to your noblest. Do not even waste time in regretting; it is weakening. Simply make up your mind: I will not do it again! And then if you fail, repeat: I will not do it again, for by so doing I alone am the loser. The day will come when, by the constant repetition of the mantram, the continuous aspiration of both the heart and the mind, and by the continuous striving or effort to be the best, the most beautiful, that is in you, you will suddenly be it, suddenly you will become it.

In living the chela life you simply exchange things that you detest inwardly, that you hate, for things that are beautiful, helpful; exchanging weakness for strength, ugliness for beauty, blindness for vision, darkness for light.

Do not struggle; do not strive; do not

fret; do not worry yourself. Be natural; be patient; be calm; be peaceful; be not impatient, be very patient. Take things as they come and strive continuously; strive after what you love best and feel to be truest, and let all the rest go. Do your duty by all, no matter at what cost to yourself, and you will find that there is an unspeakable joy in it all. Then, sooner or later, there will come the opening of the inner eye, the vision, the opening of the inner senses, the becoming cognizant of the most wonderful and strange things around you.

The spiritual faculties are within you, and can be cultivated to an infinite extent. When the inner eye is opened you shall have spiritual clairvoyance — vision of universal sweep, limited only so far as you as an individual can interpret, can receive, can contain — and the spiritual ability to see and to see aright; and in seeing to know that your seeing is truth. When you have allied yourself with the god within you, the spiritual power will show you how to see things at whatever

THE CHELA PATH 143

distance. You immediately see things at enormous distances through the inner spiritual eye. Your consciousness is there, whither you have cast it. You can sit in your armchair and see, with eyes closed, all that you care to see at great distances. This can be done not only in this exterior world but you can penetrate into the interior and invisible worlds with this spiritual vision, and thus know what is going on in the worlds spiritual and ethereal; and remember also that these inner and invisible worlds are the basis or root of this mere cross section which we humans call the physical universe. This physical universe is just one phase or plane of the great universe of boundless life.

In Tibet this power is called the *hpho-wa*, which means the power to project your consciousness (which means also your will) to any distance that you may please: on earth, to the moon, to any other planet, to the sun. This is possible, because the cosmic spaces are your home. You are they and they are you. The very powers which work in them are also in you. The very substances out of which they are born and builded, you also are builded out of. You are native there; and therefore manifesting such a power is a natural thing to do.

Another spiritual power is true and genuine clairaudience: the ability to hear with the spiritual auditory power or faculty — the inner spiritual ear — even what the gods are saying and doing. Having this power you can hear the music of the spheres, for every celestial orb, as it swings along its pathway, sings its own majestic paean, and everything on earth or elsewhere, animate or so-called inanimate, being a collection of atoms, is therefore a symphonic melody, a symphony, the aggregated volume of sound being composed of the notes of each and every singing entity, and every atom thereof is a singing entity, so that our physical bodies themselves are imbodied song.

Every little atom is attuned to a musical note. It is in constant movement, in constant vibration at speeds which are incomprehen-

THE CHELA PATH 145

sible to the ordinary brain-mind of man; and each such speed has its own numerical quantity, in other words, its own numerical note, and therefore sings that note; so that had you this spiritual clairaudience, the life surrounding you would be one grand sweet song and you yourself would sing a song, your very body would be, as it were, a symphonic orchestra, singing some magnificent, incomprehensible, musical symphonic composition.

With the awakened power of the inner spiritual ear you would hear as a song the opening of the rosebud, and its growth would be like a changing melody running along from day to day. You could hear the green grass-blade grow. You could hear every hair on your head as it lengthens in growth, for growth is movement. The growth of a little child you would hear as a prolonged chorus of singing atomic entities.

Then, with the awakened spiritual power you can transfer your thoughts without a word — voiceless speech — and your consciousness and your will to any part of the earth and actually be there, see what goes on, and know what is happening there.

Another spiritual faculty is the awakened understanding: the faculty which enables you to discriminate between thoughts and thoughts, things and things, to know one from the other. It is a sister of almighty love: for understanding is also of the very nature of the heart of the universe. You have it within you. You can understand all things if you cultivate it: why the grass grows, why the bloom is on the peach, why your fellow human beings live, why you are here, what the stars in their courses are constantly singing to you, why hate and love, night and day, summer and winter, heat and cold, and all the other pairs of opposites, exist in the universe.

But the greatest faculty, the greatest power of all is that, when you have found yourself, when you have begun to know yourself, you will discover within you incomprehensible mysteries, beautiful, sublime, indescribable, grand; and the most wonderful of them all is the power of almighty love, for this is the very cement of the universe, which holds all things in steady, orderly, sequential courses — nature's supremest, grandest power; and nothing in the heavens above, or in the earth beneath, or in the regions under the earth, can stay its passage or forbid its penetrating power. It is all-permeant, it penetrates everywhere, and when you radiate love you produce love in others, because you yourself become lovely, because of its irradiating influences arising in your own heart. Becoming one with it — with what you are within your own inner being — you become a god, a very god, for such a god you are in your inmost — Son of the Sun in very truth. The divinity within you is a glory, a glory which is indescribable, shining, splendid, emanating spiritual energy and power all the time.

Thus the powers you should cultivate in order to grow, to be, to succeed, are those which nothing can withstand, which nothing and none can resist, which work day and night, in the silence and in the storm, always zealously, the very heart-energy of the universe, of which you are a child. It is these powers which you should cultivate: love, intelligence, compassion, pity, forgiveness, and such fruits of these as are gentleness, kindheartedness, mildness of spirit. For you never can obtain these spiritual powers until every vestige of the selfish selfhood is washed out of you; for nature will not allow it. The very way by which to gain wondrous powers is by giving up the selfhood which prevents those powers from acting.

Therefore I say to you: go to the sun within you, take the kingdom of heaven by violence for it is yours, it is your spiritual heritage.

There are dangers that beset the path of the chela, but he learns how to act so as to overcome them. He learns to understand and therefore to feel that, as he becomes like unto the gods, he must follow godlike ways. He has a free will. Having this free will it is his bounden duty to exercise it; and in exercising it, he is bound to exercise it always in impersonal ways and for impersonal objects; and the greater the degree in which the chela can do this, the more quickly does he advance along the path. The higher one goes, the more necessary is it to forget self progressively ever more and to work in harmony with nature's laws.

When the chela acts through and by his spiritual nature alone, he becomes at one with nature and therefore works with her, and nature regards him as one of her creators and follows him obediently. Hence, because he works with nature there is no reaction from nature upon him, and thus the chela rises above karma and becomes at one with the heart of the universe, doing nothing contrary to natural law; consequently there is no reaction. He works with nature, because he is at one with the impulses of his own heart.

The higher you go along the evolutionary pathway, the more careful must you be; therefore you should be most careful of what you think and feel, and of the acts that you do. You have learned, at least in some degree, how to use your will, and what will be the result of it, and nature will hold you correspondingly responsible. As the law of the universe stands, you either rise or fall by every thought that you have and by every act that you do. At every instant of human existence you stand at a parting of the ways — the right hand or the left.

Take no thought of the consequences. Think only of doing the duty and doing it well, and let the rest go. That is the road of peace, the road of happiness, the road leading ever more and more upward.

A self-conscious feeling of personal or individual spiritual superiority is an actual danger. Wrench this feeling from your heart and cast it forever from you. It is a serpent which will bite and sting your inner life. Be impersonal!

For the greatest of dangers is the sense of spiritual pride. Cast it out and work on yourself until you purge your heart of its

THE CHELA PATH 151

pride of egoism. Desire and pride are sometimes mistaken for intuition and the sense of one's real fitness.

And yet, it is the desire to know, not for yourself or even for the mere sake of knowing in an abstract sense, but for the sake of laying knowledge on the altar of service, which leads to advancement on the path. Oh, the immense power behind this thought and fact! It is this desire for impersonal service which purifies the heart, clarifies the mind, and impersonalizes the knots of the lower selfhood, so that they open and thereby become capable of receiving wisdom. It is this desire which is the impelling force, the driving engine, carrying the disciple forward ever higher and higher.

It is only the personal self, the lower self, that hinders progress. Reflect upon it! Remember that it is the veils of selfhood, the selfish longings, the selfish impulses, the desire to be and to achieve for self, which hinder progress. Have no desires! Do not even long to succeed! Be crystal clear in your mind, as impersonal as the spirit which is the root of you.

Do not long for light; be not agitated and anxious or even eager to advance. Avoid all emotional disturbances of any kind, even those of a higher kind. Instead, be collected; be calm; keep your mind pellucid as a mountain lake and your soul unruffled by any passing breeze of thoughts of self.

Quiet are the places where growth takes place. Still are the chambers where light enters the heart. Nature's most majestic processes are silent, peaceful, quiet. All growth is quiet, and takes place without striving, in the silence. Battle, strife, activity, hustle, bustle — all these things are signs of human imperfections, and of a lack of knowledge of the wisdom of the heart doctrine. It is indeed the way of heaven not to strive. Therefore do your work quietly, efficiently, easily. Be still and grow; be as active spiritually as you are quiet outwardly. Then your mind will reflect the golden splendor from the sun of light within yourself, your

THE CHELA PATH 153

inner god. The only thing that prevents your receiving this light is the enshrouding veils of selfhood: selfishness, egoism, anger, hate, envy, and ignoble desires of all kinds. These things the disciple must be taught to face and to kill in himself; if he does not, they will kill him.

Has it never occurred to you to resist a favorite temptation and to overcome it, and to look down at the slain self, the ugly thing that formerly had you in its grip, and wonder how you could ever have been the victim of something so vile?

Lift your soul in quiet thought upward. Love will guide the wings of your soul to your spiritual sun. Strive not; nevertheless advance. Be not anxious to achieve; nevertheless work to achieve. Blind not yourself by anxiety nor enfeeble your steps with longing; nevertheless go ahead, move, advance. Be at peace.

Refine your thoughts; cleanse your mind; purify your heart. A pure heart and an eager intellect will carry you through everything.

A love for all beings and things, both great and small, will form a rampart, a protecting wall, about you, so strong and impenetrable that nothing will reach your heart beneath that wall of love. Carve your way by your will — the mystical sword — and thus forge ahead.

Your spiritual will is not only your buckler of salvation, but it is the sword, so to say, with which you can hew your way to self-conquest, which means peace, and wisdom, and love, and bliss.

Behold the truth before you: an eager intellect, an open mind, an unveiled spiritual vision, perception of truth, the spiritual will evoked and active so that you become supreme *first over yourself*, so that thus you have absolute self-command, and so that even the elementals and the elementaries of the astral world cannot in any wise control you. Know yourself, control yourself, and then you will be a master of life.

You cannot study this inner spiritual life of you too intensively. It is compact of truth, of almighty love, of compassion, of pity, of all the elements in the universe which produce, through the intelligence and hearts of men, kindliness, brotherhood, gentleness, and things of good and high report. This study of our spiritual being shows us that we must break through the enshrouding veils of the lower selfhood and penetrate within to the divinity, to the inner god, which is the heart of the heart of each one of us. Then, when we have reached that sublime goal, we shall have the impulse to turn around, as do the glorious Buddhas of Compassion who turn backward on the path, and help our fellows trailing along behind. This compassionate act is what all true spiritual saviors of men do.

The Buddhas of Compassion

VII

The Buddhas of Compassion

IT IS the Great Ones, the masters of life, whose light illumines the pathway, even at its commencement, and grows brighter with each step. Their light shines continuously; and it is only the dark clouds in the minds of men that shut it out. These are the Buddhas of Compassion.

A Buddha is one who has ascended the rungs of the evolutionary ladder of life, rung by rung, one after the other, and who thus has attained Buddhahood, which means human plenitude of spiritual and intellectual glory, and who has done all this by his own self-devised and self-directed exertions along the far past evolutionary pathway. He is an "Awakened One," one who manifests the divinity which is the very core of the core of his own being.

The Buddhas of Compassion are the noblest flowers of the human race. They are men who have raised themselves from humanity into quasi-divinity; and this is done by letting the light imprisoned within, the light of the inner god, pour forth and manifest itself through the humanity of the man, through the human soul of the man. Through sacrifice and abandoning of all that is mean and wrong, ignoble and paltry and selfish; through opening up the inner nature so that the god within may shine forth; in other words, through self-directed evolution, they have raised themselves from mere manhood into becoming god-men, man-gods — human divinity.

Every human being is a Buddha unmanifest. Every human being has, in his inner constitution, not only the Celestial Buddha, the Dhyāni-Buddha, which is his inner god, but his higher ego, which when expressing itself on earth as a man, is the Mānushya-

Buddha or Human Buddha. Ordinary men cannot fully and wholly manifest the powers of their higher spiritual will or ego, because ordinary men are too gross; they as vehicles are not yet sufficiently etherealized. They live too much in the planes of material being. They are passional; they are personal, consequently circumscribed, limited.

Every human being is an unexpressed Buddha. Even now, within you and above you, it is your higher self, and your higher self is it; and as the ages pass and as you conquer the self in order to become the greater self, you approach with every step nearer and nearer to the "sleeping" Buddha within you. And yet truly it is not the Buddha which is "asleep"; it is you who are sleeping on the bed of matter, dreaming evil dreams, brought about by your passions, by your false views, by your egoisms, by your selfishness — making thick and heavy veils of personality wrapping around the Buddha within.

For here is the secret: the Buddha within

you is watching you. Your own inner Buddha has his eye, mystically speaking, on you. His hand is reached compassionately downward toward you, so to speak, but you must reach up and clasp that hand by your own unaided will and aspiration — you, the human part of you — and take the hand of the Buddha within you.

A strange figure of speech? Consider then what a human being is: a god in the heart of him, a Buddha enshrining that god, a spiritual soul enshrining the Buddha, a human soul enshrining the spiritual soul, an animal soul enshrining the human soul, and a body enshrining the animal soul. So that man is at the same time one, and many more than one.

When a human being has learned all that earth can teach him, he is then godlike and returns to earth no more — except those whose hearts are so filled with the holy flame of compassion that they remain in the school-room of earth that they have long since advanced beyond and where they themselves can learn nothing more, in order to help their younger, less evolved brothers. These exceptions are the Buddhas of Compassion.

There are, on the other hand, very great men, very holy men, very pure men in every way, whose knowledge is wide and vast and deep, whose spiritual stature is great; but when they reach Buddhahood, instead of feeling the call of almighty love to return and help those who have gone less far, they go ahead into the supernal light — pass onwards and enter the unspeakable bliss of nirvana — and leave mankind behind. Such are the Pratyeka Buddhas. Though exalted, nevertheless they do not rank in unutterable sublimity with the Buddhas of Compassion.

The Pratyeka Buddha, he who achieves Buddhahood for himself, does not do it selfishly, however; does not do it merely in order to gratify self, and he does no harm to others; if he did he could never reach even his solitary Buddhahood. But he does it and achieves nirvana automatically, so to speak, following the lofty impulses of his being.

Nevertheless he leaves the world behind enslaved in the chains of matter and forgotten by him.

The Pratyeka Buddha concentrates on the one thing — self-advancement for spiritual ends. It is a noble path in a way, but although it is a more rapid path, nevertheless being essentially a selfish path, the karmic records will show deeper lines ultimately to be wiped out than will those of the other striver after the spiritual life who follows the path of complete self-renunciation, and who even gives up all hope of self-advancement. The latter is of course by far the nobler path, but for a time it is very much slower, and much more difficult to follow. The objective, the end, is more difficult to obtain; but when obtained, then the guerdon, the reward, the recompense, are ineffably sublime. For a time it is a slower path, but a perfect path.

It is a wonderful paradox that is found in the case of the Pratyeka Buddha — this name *pratyeka* means "each for himself." But this spirit of "each for himself" is just the opposite of the spirit governing the Order of the Buddhas of Compassion, because in the Order of Compassion the spirit is: give up thy life for all that lives.

The "Solitary One" knows that he cannot advance to spiritual glory unless he live the spiritual life, unless he cultivate his spiritual nature, but as he does this solely in order to win spiritual rewards, spiritual life, for himself alone, he is a Pratyeka Buddha. He is *for himself,* in the last analysis. There is a personal eagerness, a personal wish, to forge ahead, to attain at any cost; whereas he who belongs to the Order of the Buddhas of Compassion has his eyes set on the same distant objective, but he trains himself from the very beginning to become utterly self-forgetful. This obviously is an enormously greater labor, and of course the rewards are correspondingly great.

The time comes when the Pratyeka Buddha, holy as he is, noble in effort and in ideal as he is, reaches a state of development where he can go no farther on that path. But, contrariwise, the one who allies himself from the very beginning with all nature, and with nature's heart, has a constantly expanding field of work, as his consciousness expands and fills that field; and this expanding field is simply illimitable, because it is boundless nature herself. He becomes utterly at one with the spiritual universe; whereas the Pratyeka Buddha becomes at one with only a particular line or stream of evolution in the universe.

The Pratyeka Buddha raises himself to the spiritual realm of his own inner being, enwraps himself therein and, so to speak, goes to sleep. The Buddha of Compassion raises himself, as does the Pratyeka Buddha, to the spiritual realms of his own inner being, but does not stop there, because he expands continuously, becomes one with All, or tries to, and in fact does so in time.

The Buddha of Compassion is one who having won all, gained all, gained the right to cosmic peace and bliss, renounces it so that he may go back as a Son of Light in order to help humanity, and indeed all that is. The Pratyeka Buddha passes onwards and enters the unspeakable bliss of nirvana, and there he remains for an aeon or a million of aeons as the case may be; whereas the Buddha of Compassion, who has renounced all for compassion's sake, because his heart is so filled with love, continues evolving. Thus the time comes when the Buddha of Compassion, although having renounced everything, will have advanced far beyond the state that the Pratyeka Buddha has reached; and when the Pratyeka Buddha in due course emerges from the nirvanic state in order to take up his evolutionary journey again, he will find himself far in the rear of the Buddha of Compassion.

Self, selfhood, self-seeking, is the very thing that the Buddhas of Compassion strive to forget, to overcome, to live beyond. The self personal must blend into the self individual, which then must lose itself in the self universal.

They are called Buddhas of Compassion because they feel their unity with all that is, and more and more so as they evolve, until finally their consciousness blends with the universe and lives eternally and immortally, because it is at one with the universe. The dewdrop slips into the shining sea — its origin.

Feeling the urge of almighty love in their hearts, the Buddhas of Compassion advance forever steadily towards still greater heights of spiritual achievement; and the reason is that they have become the vehicles of universal love. As impersonal love is universal, their whole nature expands consequently with the universal powers that are working through them.

Strive not to become holy for yourself. Strive to become holy as others strive to become holy, but only that you can forget yourself for others. Love never seeks self for self. Love always seeks to give. Love is the first step on the upward way. It is all intermediate steps and it is the last, if indeed there be a last. Love is also the last and highest initiation on earth — impersonal love, for such love is divine.

THE BUDDHAS OF COMPASSION 169

The Mahatmas are not yet Buddhas. A Buddha is a Mahatma of the highest grade. A Mahatma is one who has become self-consciously alive in the spiritual part of his constitution, whereas a Buddha is one who has become self-consciously living in the divine-spiritual part of his constitution.

The Masters are human beings, although lofty ones, and it is this that makes them so near and dear to us. They occupy the step immediately superior to ordinary humanity. They are soul-men in human bodies, feeling as men feel, understanding human woes and human sorrows, capable of cognizing what human failings and human sin are, and therefore having human hearts moved with tender compassion and pity. They know also the need, when occasion arises, of the strong and directing hand. They are brothers, tender-hearted men, great-hearted men, of magnificent spiritual and intellectual powers and faculties.

"Diamond-heart" is the term used when speaking of the Mahatma; and it has its symbolic meaning, signifying the crystal-clear consciousness reflecting the misery of the world, receiving and reflecting the call for help, reflecting the Buddhic splendor in the heart of every struggling soul on earth; but yet as hard as the diamond for all calls of the personality, the self-personality, and first of all of the Mahatma's own personal nature.

Should the Mahatma abandon his physical body and live in his other principles, he becomes de facto a *Nirmāṇakāya*, living in the auric atmosphere of the earth and working for mankind invisibly, thus becoming one of the living stones in the Guardian Wall.

The Nirmāṇakāya is a complete man possessing all the principles of his constitution, except the *liṅga-śarīra*, and its accompanying physical body. He lives on the plane of being next superior to the physical plane, and his purpose in so doing is to save men from themselves by being with them, and by continuously instilling thoughts of self-sacrifice, of self-forgetfulness, of spiritual and moral beauty, of mutual help, of compassion, of

THE BUDDHAS OF COMPASSION 171

pity. Thus it is that he forms one of the stones in the Guardian Wall invisibly surrounding mankind.

Most Mahatmas prepare to become Buddhas of Compassion, and therefore to renounce a nirvanic state.

The real Buddha of Compassion renounces nirvana for himself in order to help the world, for he is compassion incarnate. He lives through aeons, working for all that is, advancing steadily by self-devised efforts, by self-directed evolution, towards divinity, towards godhood; and it is this utter self-sacrifice of the human being, of the most sublime and lofty type conceivable to men, which makes of a Buddha so holy and exalted a being.

The Buddha stands higher even than an Avatāra, for the Buddha is a self-chosen incarnation of wisdom and compassion, pity, love, self-forgetfulness. Sons of the Sun, the Buddhas enlighten wherever they go. They abide through the ages and form a Guardian Wall around mankind, protecting it against cosmic perils, of which perils none but high initiates know. The Lords Buddha are the holiest ones.

In the distinction between the Pratyeka Buddha and the Buddha of Compassion there enters the element of a deliberate choice which each one must someday make.

Which path will you then take, the path of the Buddhas of Compassion, or the path of the Pratyeka Buddhas? Either is noble; both lead to heights of spiritual sublimity — one the path of compassion, the path divine; the other, the path of personal rest, utter peace, bliss, and living in the divine. Some day you must make that choice. But the results of making that choice, of choosing the road of self-forgetfulness and pity and impersonal love for all others, for all things, while temporarily holding you in the realms of illusion, of matter, will ultimately lead you by a road, straighter than any other, to the very core of the core of the universal heart; for you shall have obeyed the impersonal commands of cosmic love, and that means

THE BUDDHAS OF COMPASSION 173

allying yourself consciously with divinity.

Nirvana if chosen for oneself can be looked upon as a species of sublimated spiritual selfishness: for the attempt of trying to gain nirvana for oneself alone is a solely individual yearning to free oneself from manifested life, to stand apart in utter peace and utter bliss, in pure consciousness, and without regard for anything else.

How different from this is the teaching of the Lord Buddha: "Can I remain in utter bliss when one single human heart beats in pain?" Give me rather, is the thought, the suffering of personal existence, so that I may help and comfort others instead of attaining the purely selfish bliss of individual *paranishpanna*.

Where is the sun of compassion and pity and self-forgetfulness and peace? Do not compassion and pity sway the soul?

Compassion is rooted in love. And harmony and love are fundamentally the same. Its very nature, the very structure of it, is that every part feels what every other part undergoes; and this, in its higher reaches and when expressing itself in human hearts, men call compassion.

Compassion is the very nature and fabric of the structure of the universe itself, the characteristic of its being, for compassion means "feeling with," and the universe is an organism, a vast and mighty organism, an organism seemingly without bounds, which might otherwise be called universal life-consciousness.

Compassion is the fundamental law of nature's own heart. It means becoming at one with the divine universe, with the universal life and consciousness. It means harmony; it means peace; it means bliss; it means impersonal love.

Having this vision sublime, do not shut your eyes to the misery of others, but devote your life like the Buddhas of Compassion to help all things, first by raising yourself — impersonally, not personally — so that you may help others to see the light divine.

Is there anything so beautiful, so high, so

THE BUDDHAS OF COMPASSION 175

noble, as bringing comfort to broken hearts, light to obscure minds, the teaching of men how to love, how to love and to forgive?

To bring peace to men, to give them hope, to give them light, to show them the way out of the intricate maze of material existence, to bring back to one's fellow men the knowledge of their own essential divinity as a reality — is not that a sublime work?